Beginners' Programme *to* Plectrum Guitar

(Grade-1)

♫♫♫♫♫♫♫♫♫♫♫♫♫♫♫

By
Kapil Srivastava
(Guitarmonk)

UNICORN BOOKS

Publishers
UNICORN BOOKS
F-2/16, Ansari Road, Daryaganj, New Delhi-110002
☎ 23275434, 23262683, 23262783 • Fax: 011-23257790
E-mail: info@unicornbooks.in • *Website:* www.unicornbooks.in

Branch : Mumbai
23-25, Zaoba Wadi, Thakurdwar, Mumbai-400002
☎ 022-22010941, 022-22053387
E-mail: rapidex@bom5.vsnl.net.in

ISBN 978-81-7806-222-8

Edition: 2017

Printed at : Param Offsetters, Okhla, New Delhi-110020

Preface

I have great pleasure to bring forth this book as part of my endeavour to give some sort of organisation and structure to the music education in India.

Going by my professional experience in the last two decades, I have realized that India badly needs an organized music teaching system. The non-existence of such a system is one of the factors that plagues music education in our country. Non-compulsory music education and lack of awareness are the other factors which add to its present state.

This is the first book of the four volume book series published under the same title. As there is a dearth of constructive content for study and reference on this subject, to a great extent, this book will serve the purpose. The well organized content and the exercises of this book are a first-class study material for the aspiring students of music to prepare for various examinations. Even a 5 year old learner can use this book and it will help him to achieve the desired goal in a short span of time.

It is a matter of great pride and pleasure to note that my other books on music are well received by students and readers alike across the globe. They are also introduced as text books in many schools. We reach out all the places and regions through these books and thus we would be able to serve you without our physical presence.

I thank readers, students and others for their support and patronage. Your suggestions and comments on the further improvement of this book will be thankfully acknowledged and the same will be incorporated in the next edition.

Author

Overview

THE OBJECTIVES

The primary objective of this book is to familiarise the learners with terminologies, exercises and repertoires along with the audios of the compositions. This would help the learners to get a clear perspective on various aspects of the subject.

WHOM IS THIS BOOK FOR?

The book is for complete beginners who know nothing about the instrument, the students who prepare for examinations and the teachers who train the students.

THE SPECIAL FEATURES

- It is customized into levels and can be covered very easily in 12-24 sessions maximum based on time involvement.
- It is an ideal book for teachers who help their student in constructive sessions and productive outcome.
- The book is a step-by-step guide which takes a student from one level to the next. It also inspires success at every grade via achievements which motivates students to get curious and interested in further learning.
- This book contains an audio-CD that instructs on speed and movement of tune: and it is a good reference for the learners who find difficulties in staff reading.
- It contains the basics of staff notations which is very useful information for any music beginner.
- It is a compilation of very significant compositions, rated at a global standard, essential for any music student.

- It offers finger movements which are the most important part for a quality and right learning and support to both teacher and student.
- It offers exercise, pop music repertoire, music theory and Practice Compositions

HOW WILL THIS BOOK HELP YOU?

- It can help you in going about a step-by-step and systematic learning
- A quality and constructive repertoire of songs for your personal performance.
- It instructs you on finger patterns, so as to help both teacher and student with accurate fingering.
- You can expect a basic performance from yourself and can render a medley of tunes on any platform after practicing the given tunes.
- It can assist you, to a great extent, for a performance preparation and content and, thus, it can bring out a musician in you.

Content

TOPIC	PAGE
Exercises	
Exercise – 1 to 10	1-16
Compositions	
Aura Lee	18-19
Lightly Row	20-21
Baby Boy	22-23
Beautiful Brown Eyes	24-25
Go Tell It To The Mountain	26-27
Titan	28
Long Long Ago	29-30
The Girl I Left Behind Me	31-32
Suzanna	33-34
Amazing Grace	35-36
500 Miles	37-38
Western Pop Songs Repertoire	
Everything I do	41
Words	42
My Heart Will Go On	43
Back To You	44
Right Here Waiting	45
Unbreakable	46
Truly Madly Deeply	47
I Need You	48

EXERCISES

TECHNICAL DEVELOPMENT

(An essential practice for every music student)

Exercise - 1

Right Hand Exercises

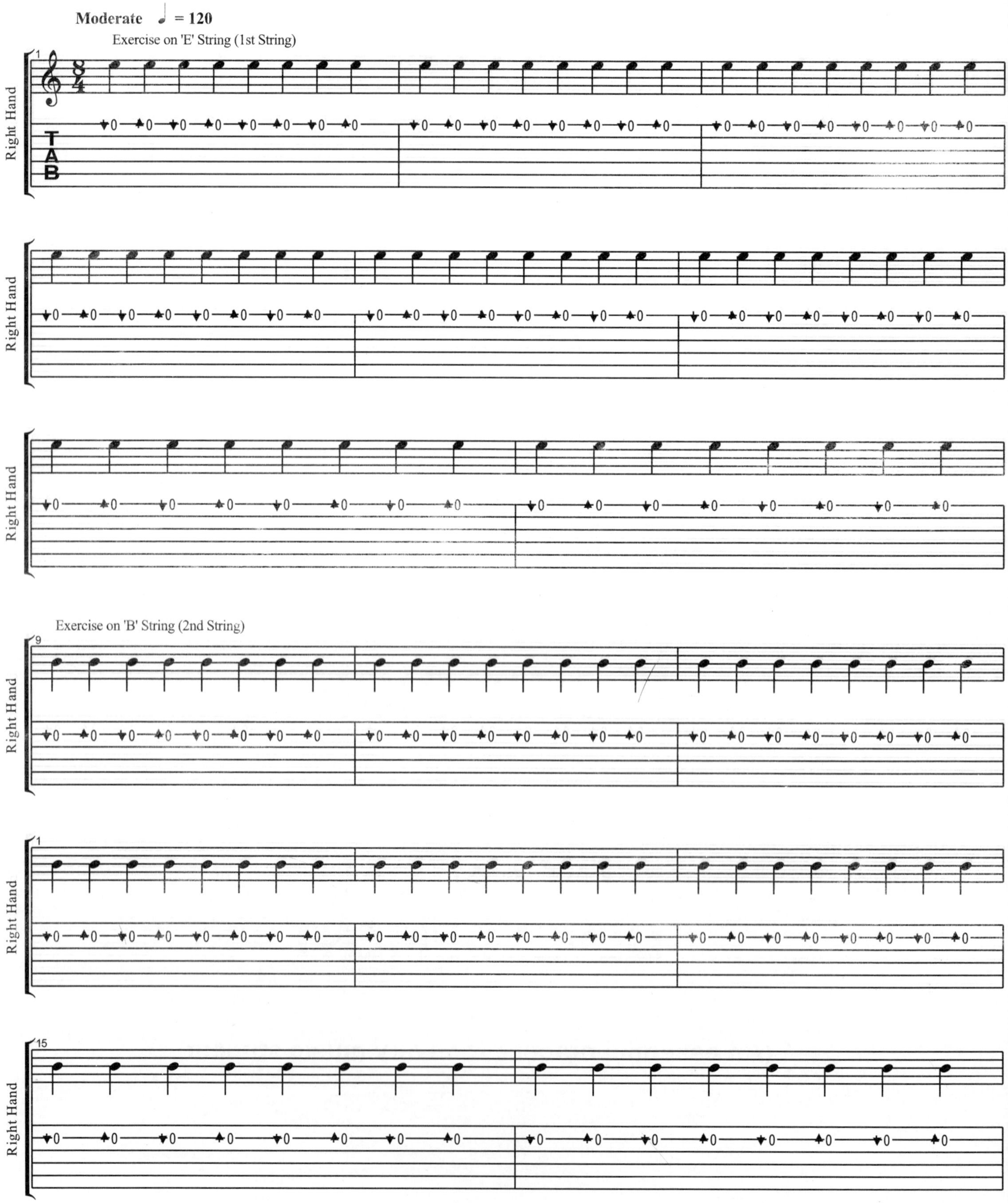

Exercise on 'G' String (3rd String)

Exercise on 'D' String (4th String)

Exercise on 'A' String (5th String)

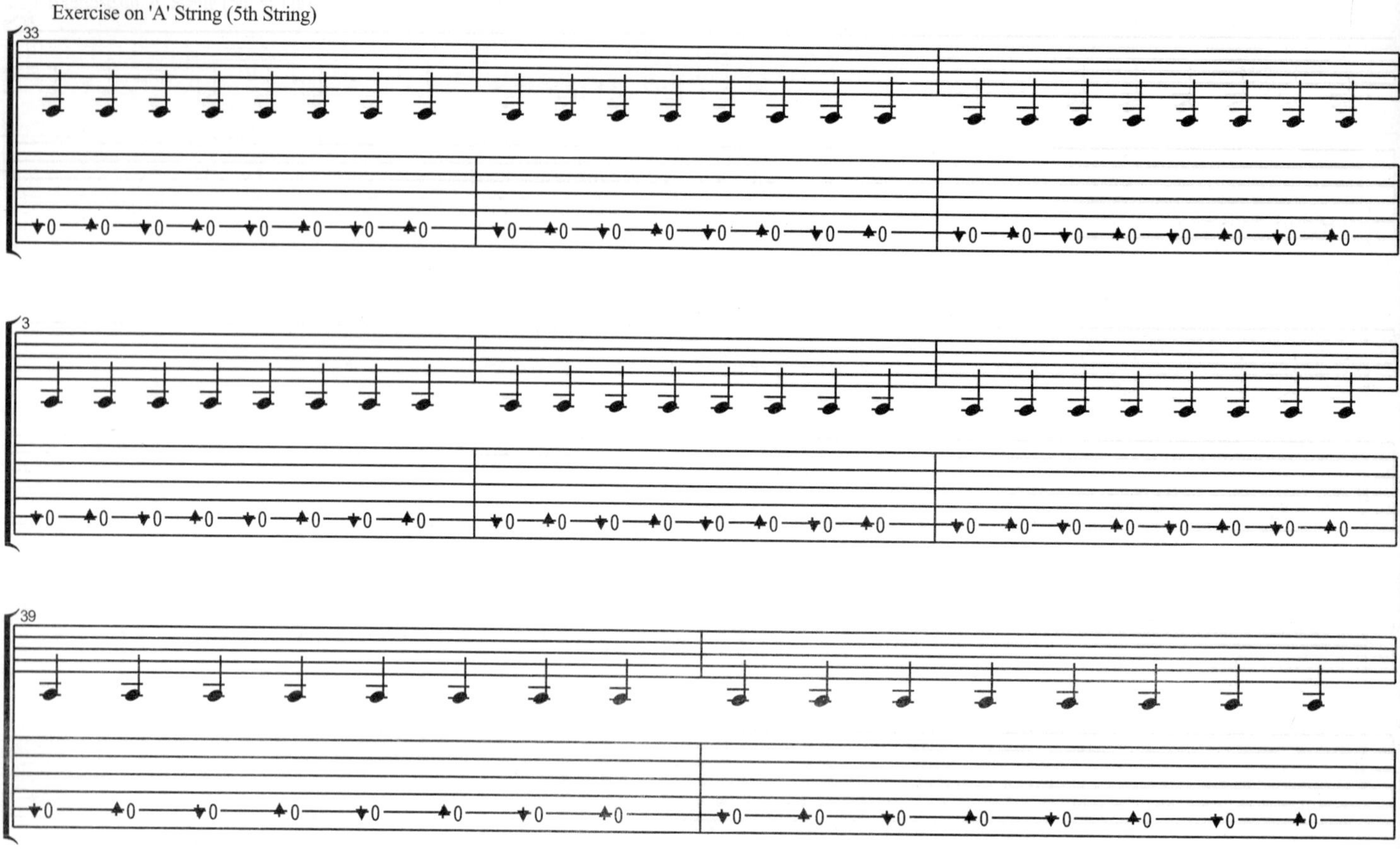

Exercise on 'E' String (6th String)

Exercise - 2

Right Hand Exercises

8 Strokes/String (Shifting Strings after every Bar/8 Strokes)

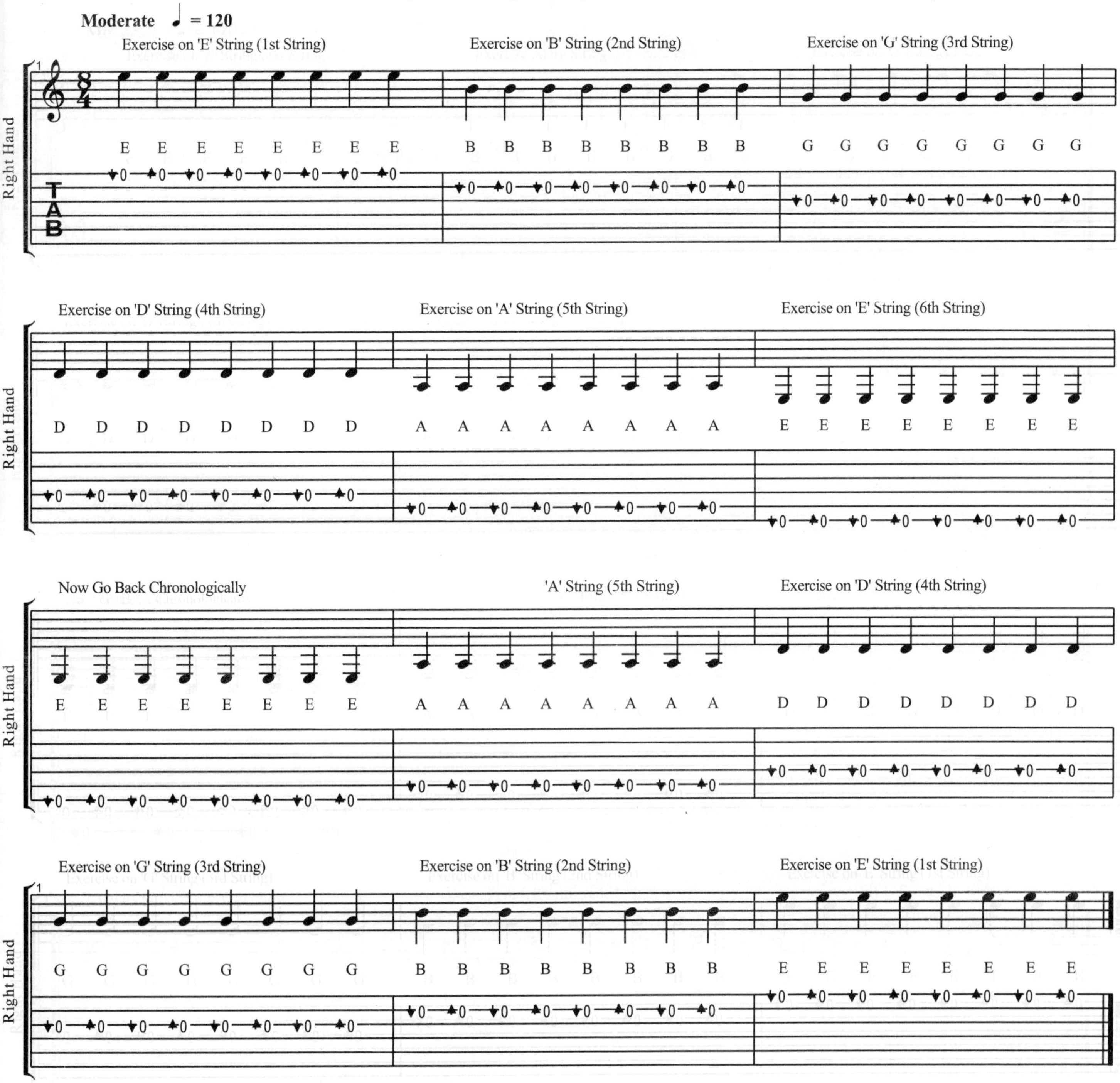

Exercise - 3

Right Hand Exercises

6 Strokes/String - (Shifting String after every Bar/6 Strokes)

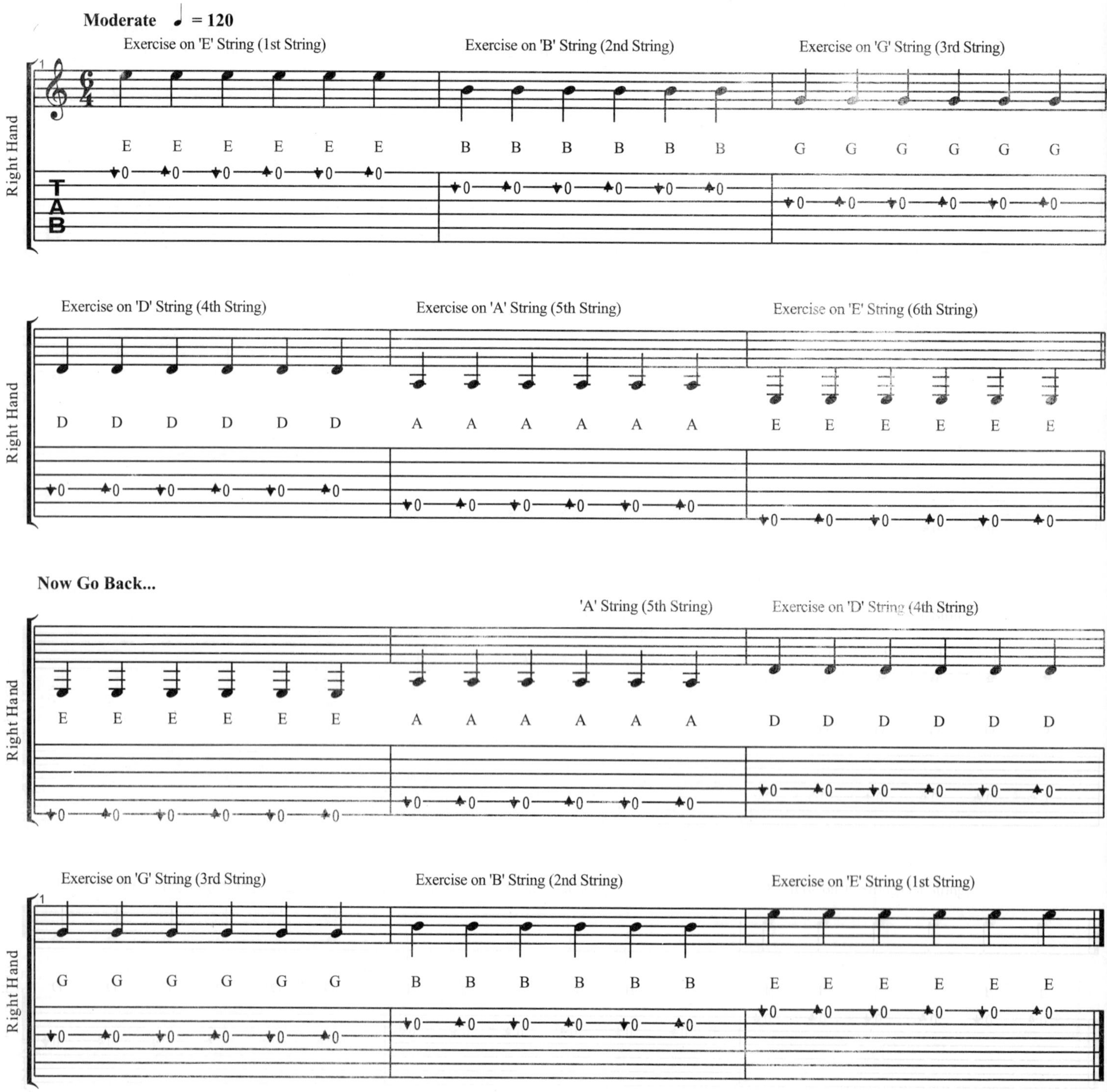

Exercise - 4

Right Hand Exercises

4 Strokes/String - (Shifting String after every Bar/4 Strokes)

Exercise - 5

Right Hand Exercises

2 Strokes/String - (Shifting String after every Bar/2 Strokes)

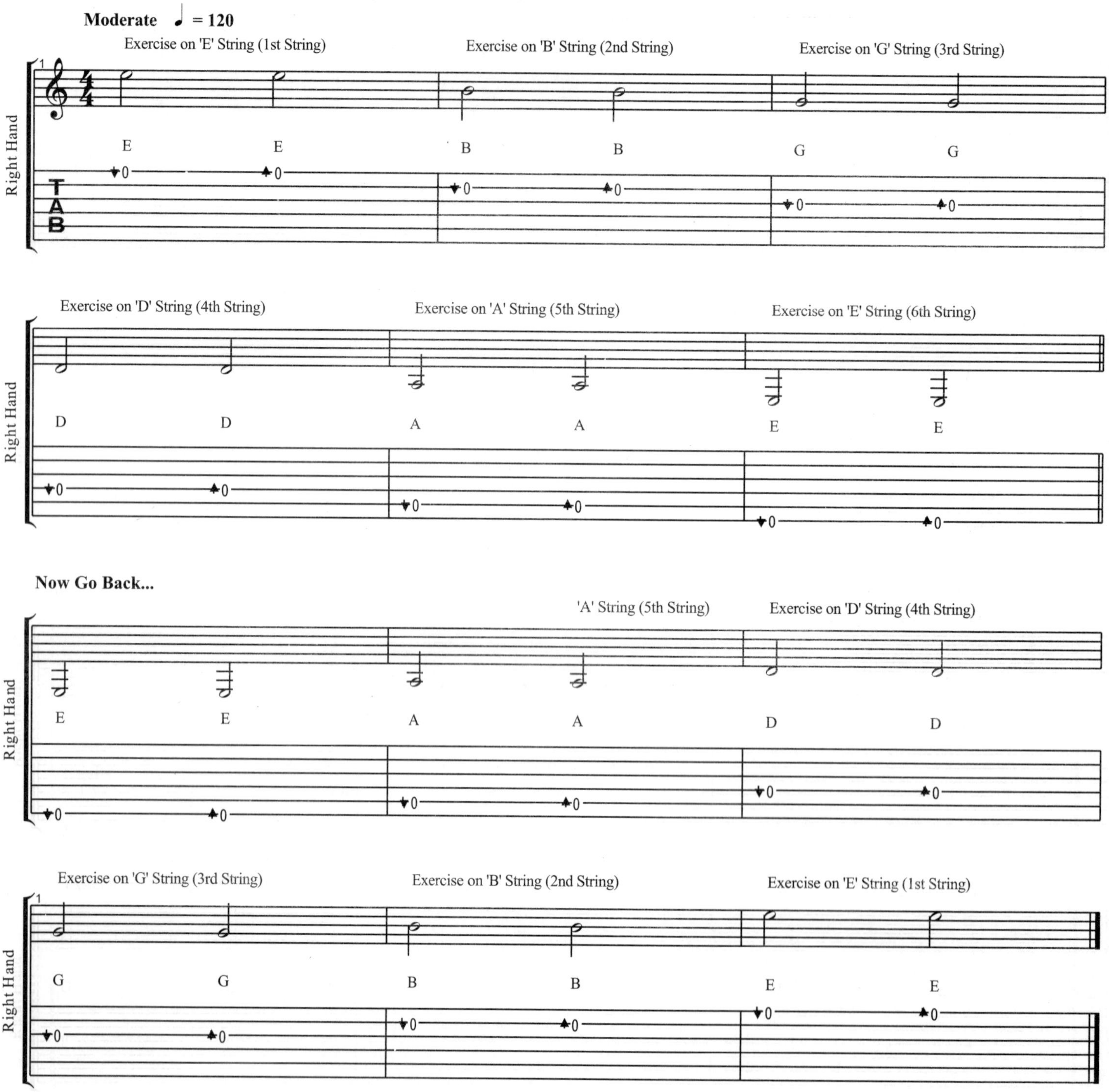

Exercise - 6

Right Hand Exercises

1 Stroke/String - (Shifting String after every 1 Stroke)

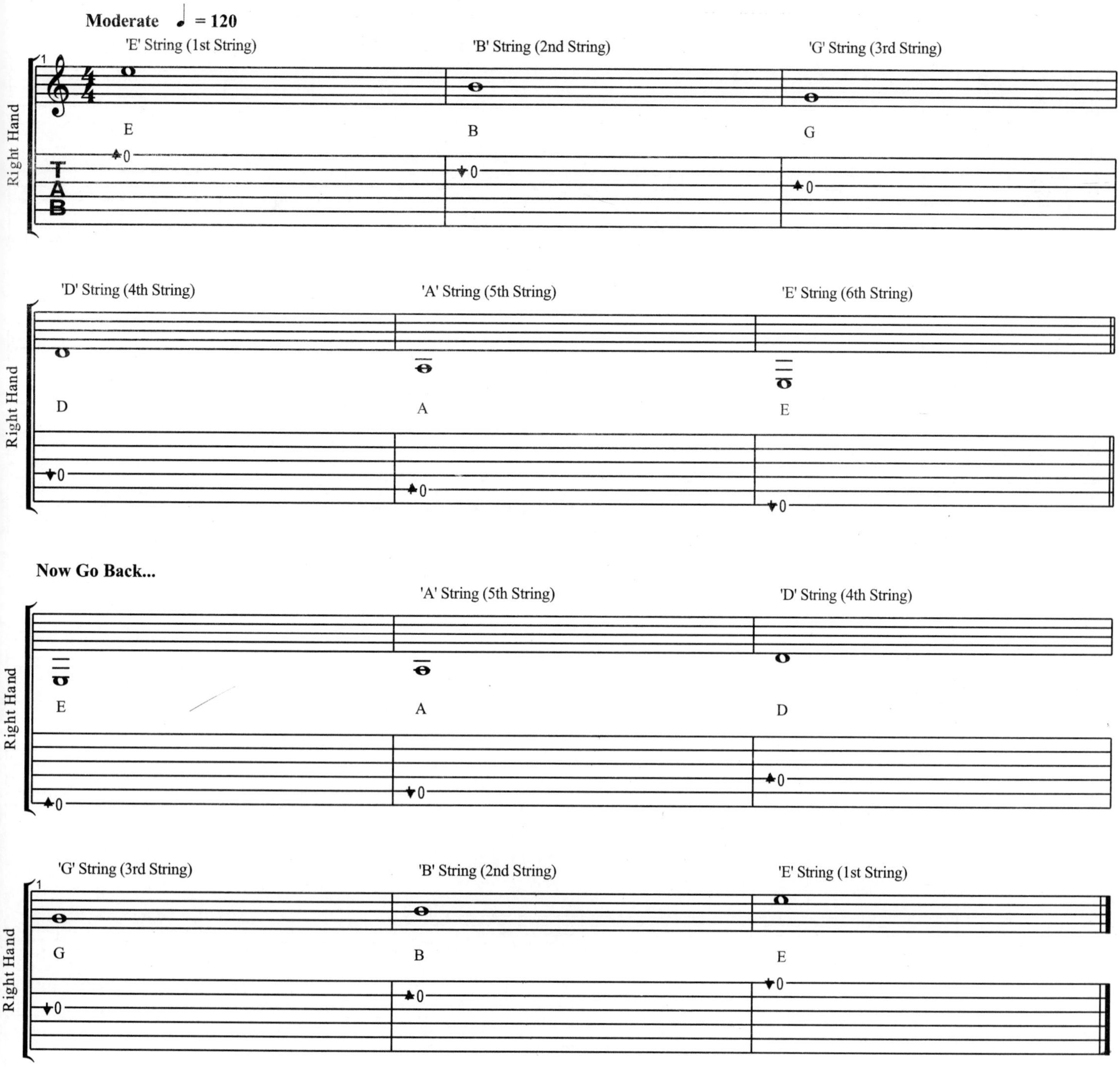

Exercise - 7

Right Hand Exercises

7 Strokes/String -(Shifting String after every Bar/7 Strokes)

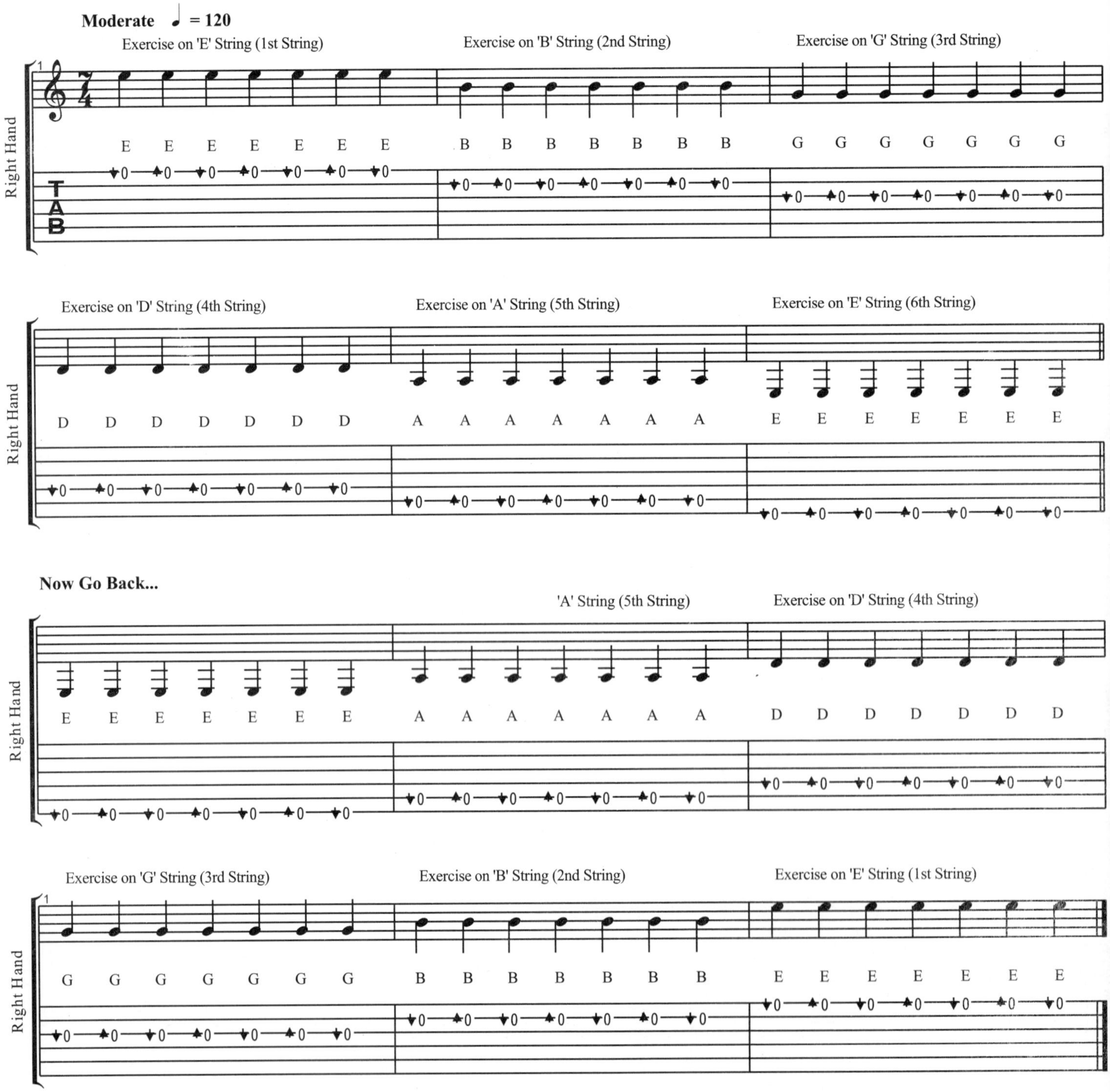

Exercise - 8

Right Hand Exercises

5 Strokes/String - (Shifting String after every Bar/5 Strokes)

Exercise - 9

Right Hand Exercises

3 Strokes/String - (Shifting String after every Bar/3 Strokes)

Exercise - 10

Right Hand Exercises

Arpeggios

Pattern in '3rd' & '5th' String
3rd
5th
Right Hand
Pattern in '4th' & '6th' String
4th
6th

6th & 4th String -- Going Back

5th & 3rd String

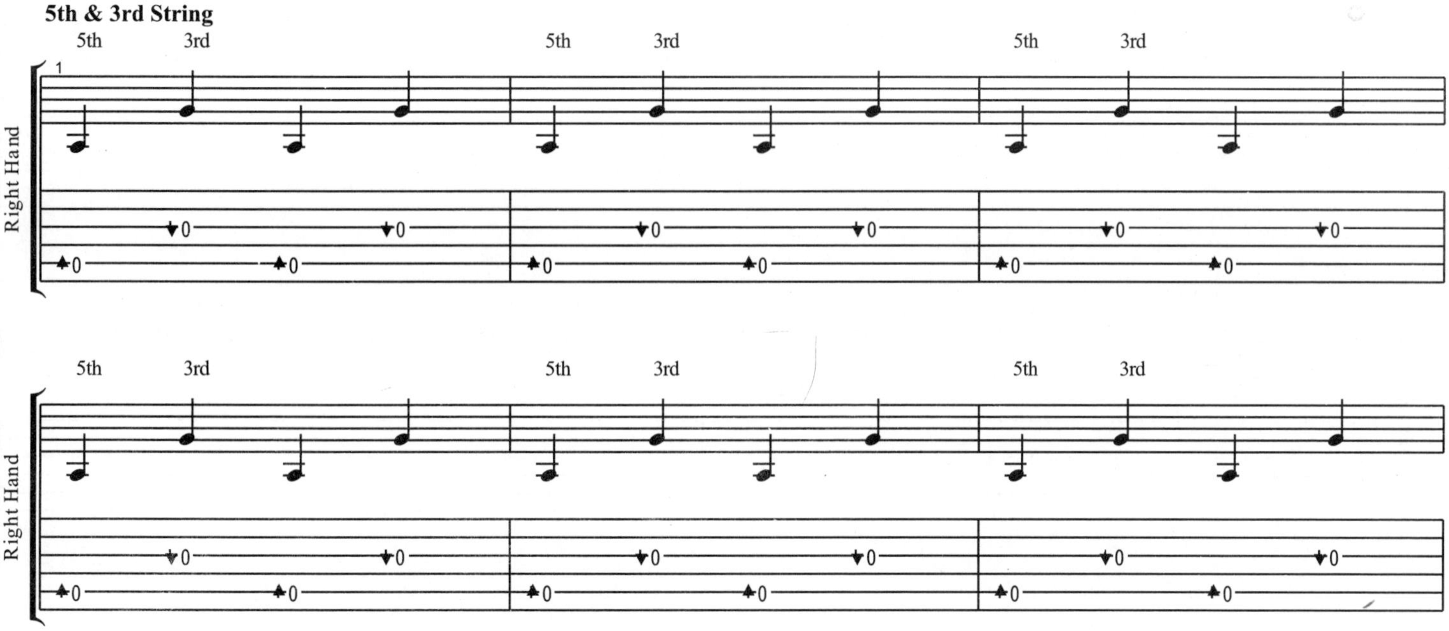

4th & 2nd String
3rd & 1st String
5th 3rd 5th 3rd 4th 2nd 4th 2nd
51
4th 2nd 4th 2nd 4th 2nd 4th 2nd
55
4th 2nd 4th 2nd 3rd 1st 3rd 1st
59
3rd 1st 3rd 1st 3rd 1st 3rd 1st
3
3rd 1st 3rd 1st
Right Hand

COMPOSITIONS

(A collection of special practice repertoire...)

Aura Lee

Plectrum Guitar, Guitarmonk

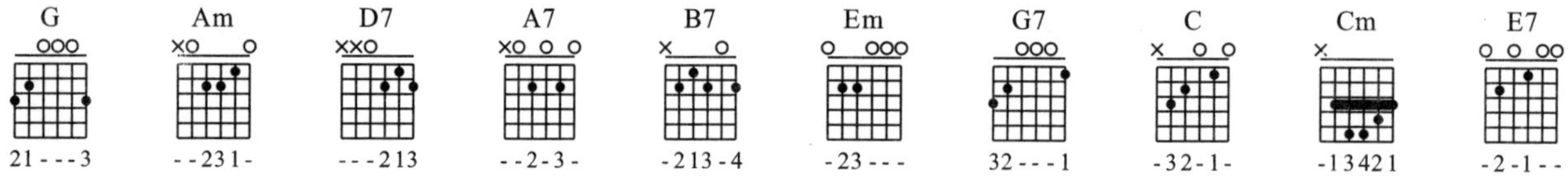

Moderate ♩ = 100

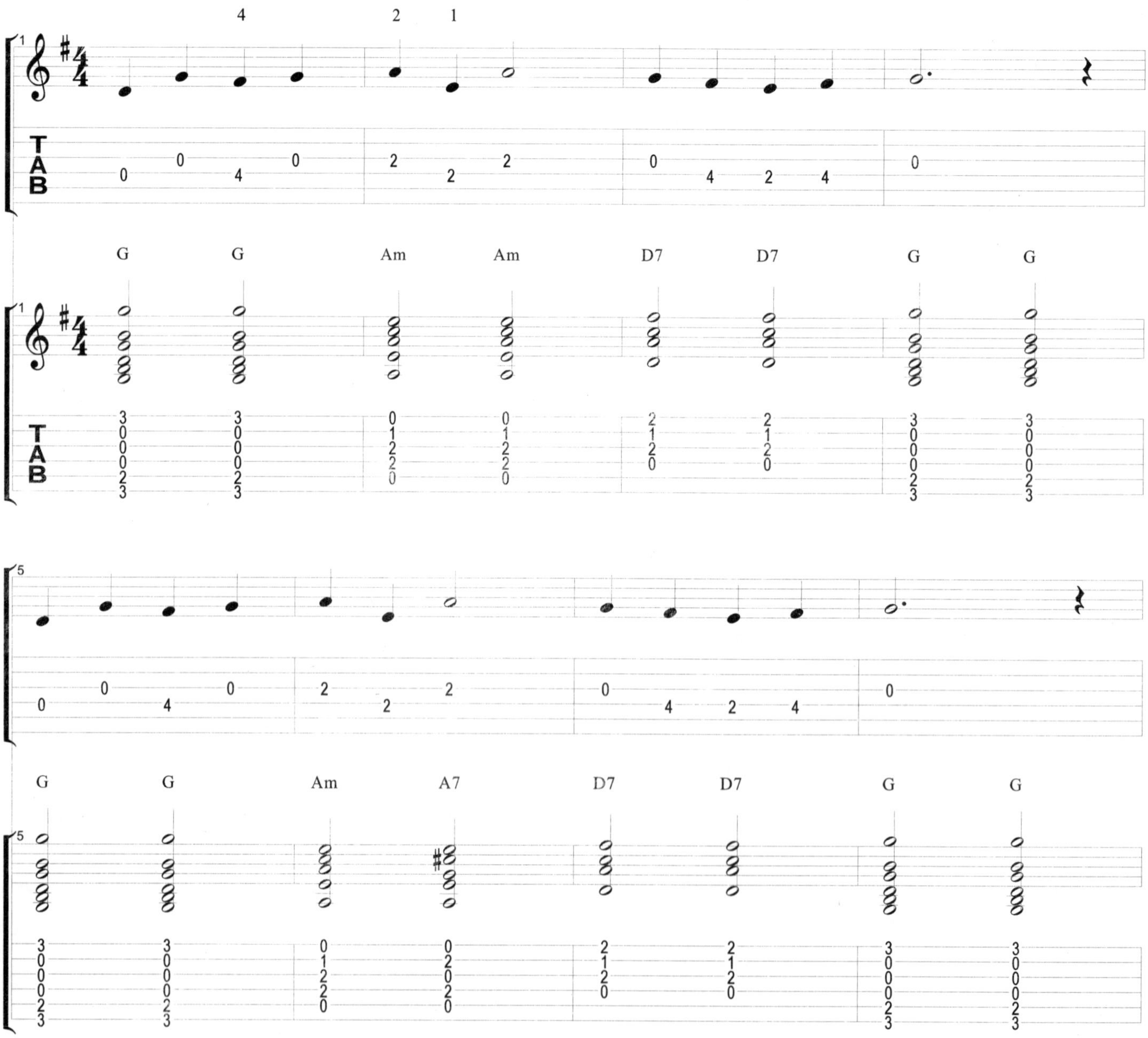

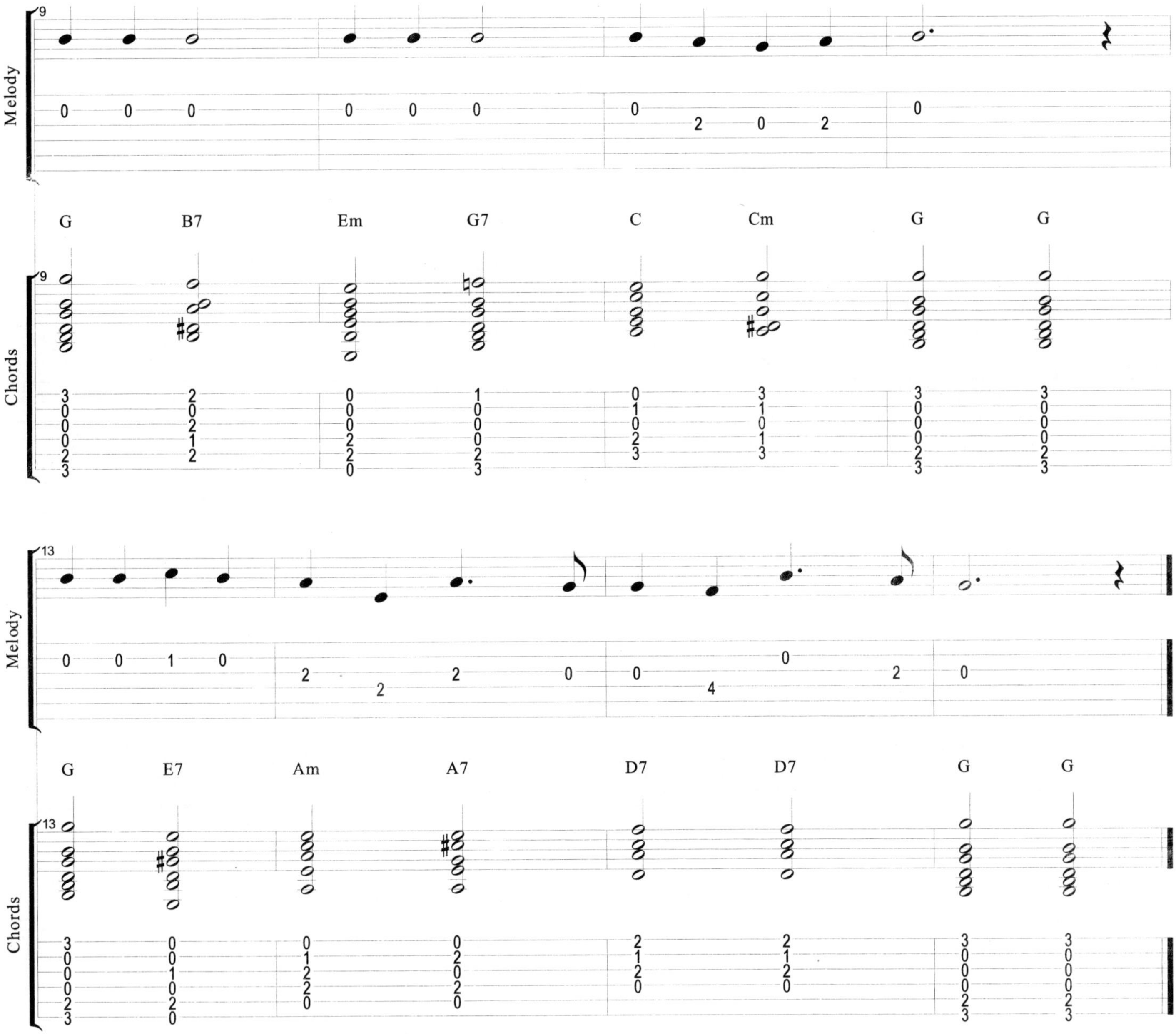
9
Melody
G B7 Em G7 C Cm G G
Chords
13
Melody
G E7 Am A7 D7 D7 G G
Chords

Lightly Row

Plectrum Guitar, Guitarmonk

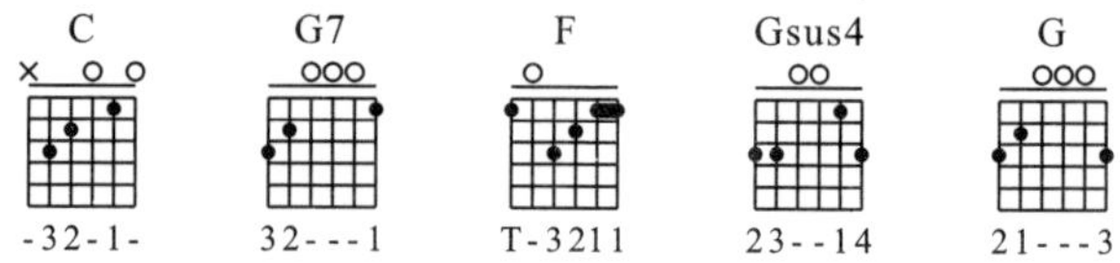

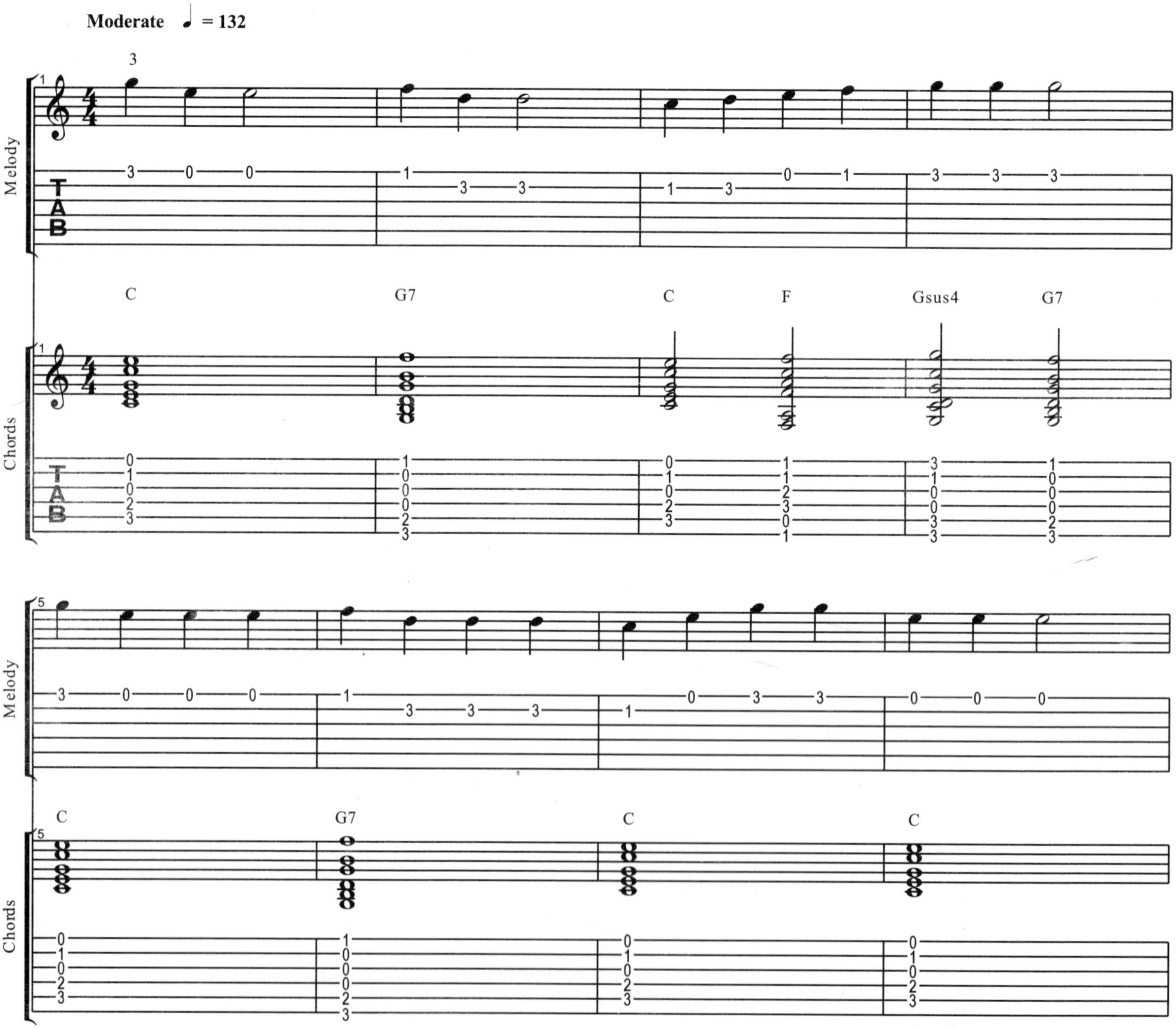

9
Melody
G
G7
C
F
G7
Chords
13
Melody
C
G
C
G7
C
Chords

Baby Boy

Plectrum Guitar, Guitarmonk

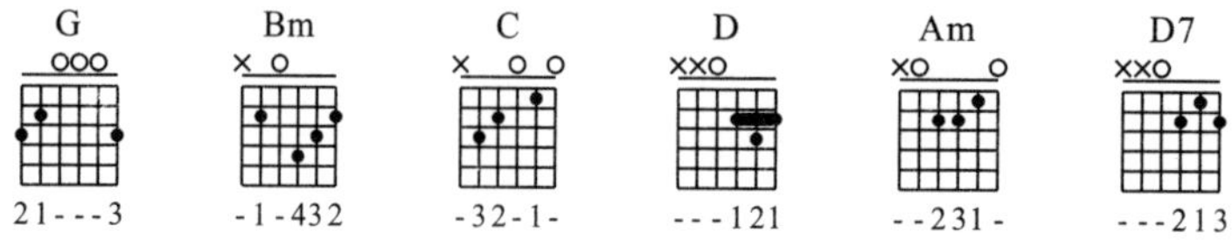

Moderate ♩ = 120

9
Melody
G D G C G G G G Bm Bm C C G G G G
Chords
13
Melody
G D G C G G G G Bm Bm C D7 G
Chords

Beautiful Brown Eyes

Plectrum Guitar, Guitarmonk

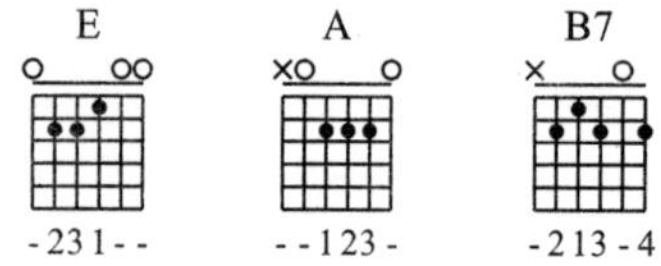

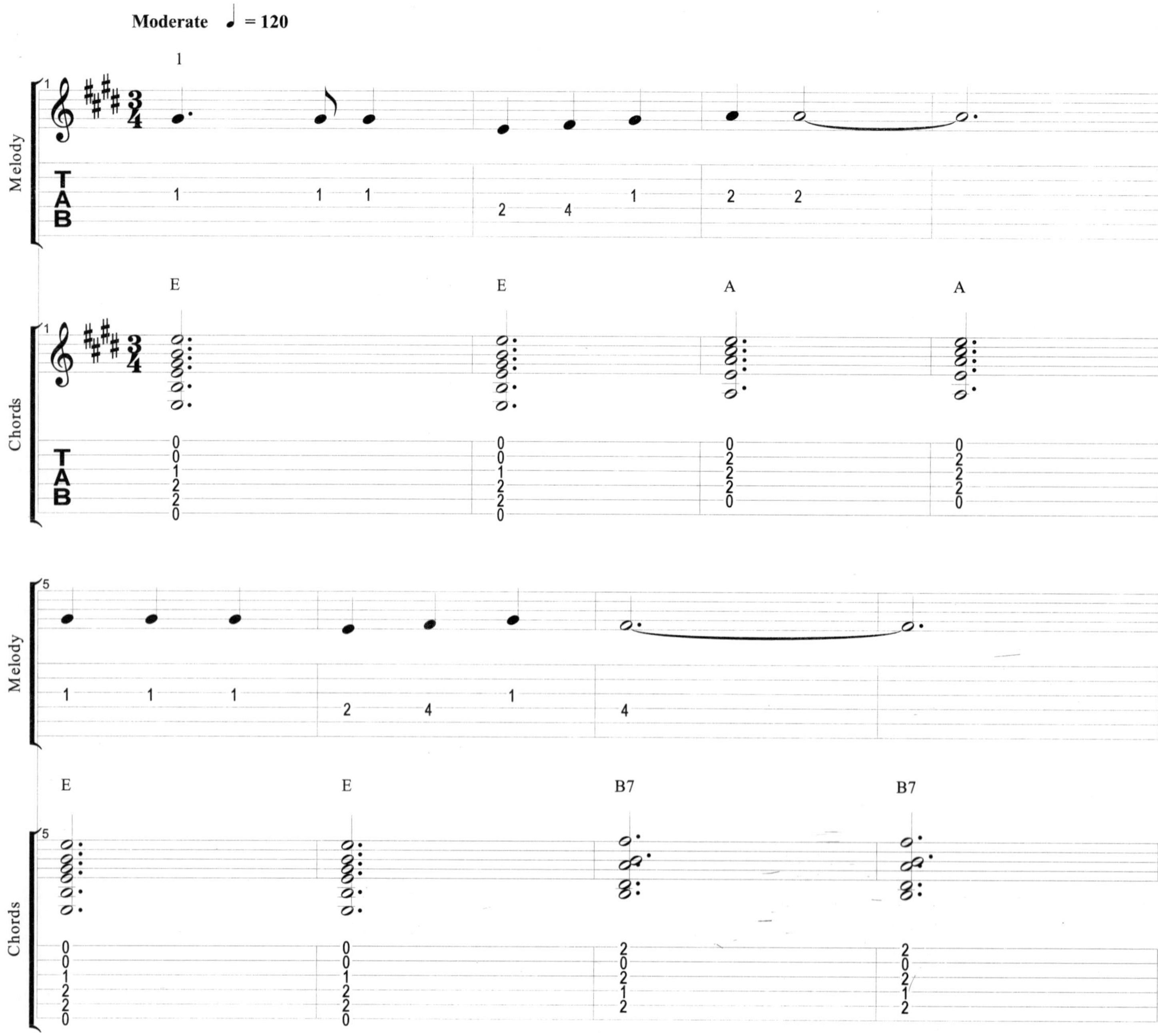

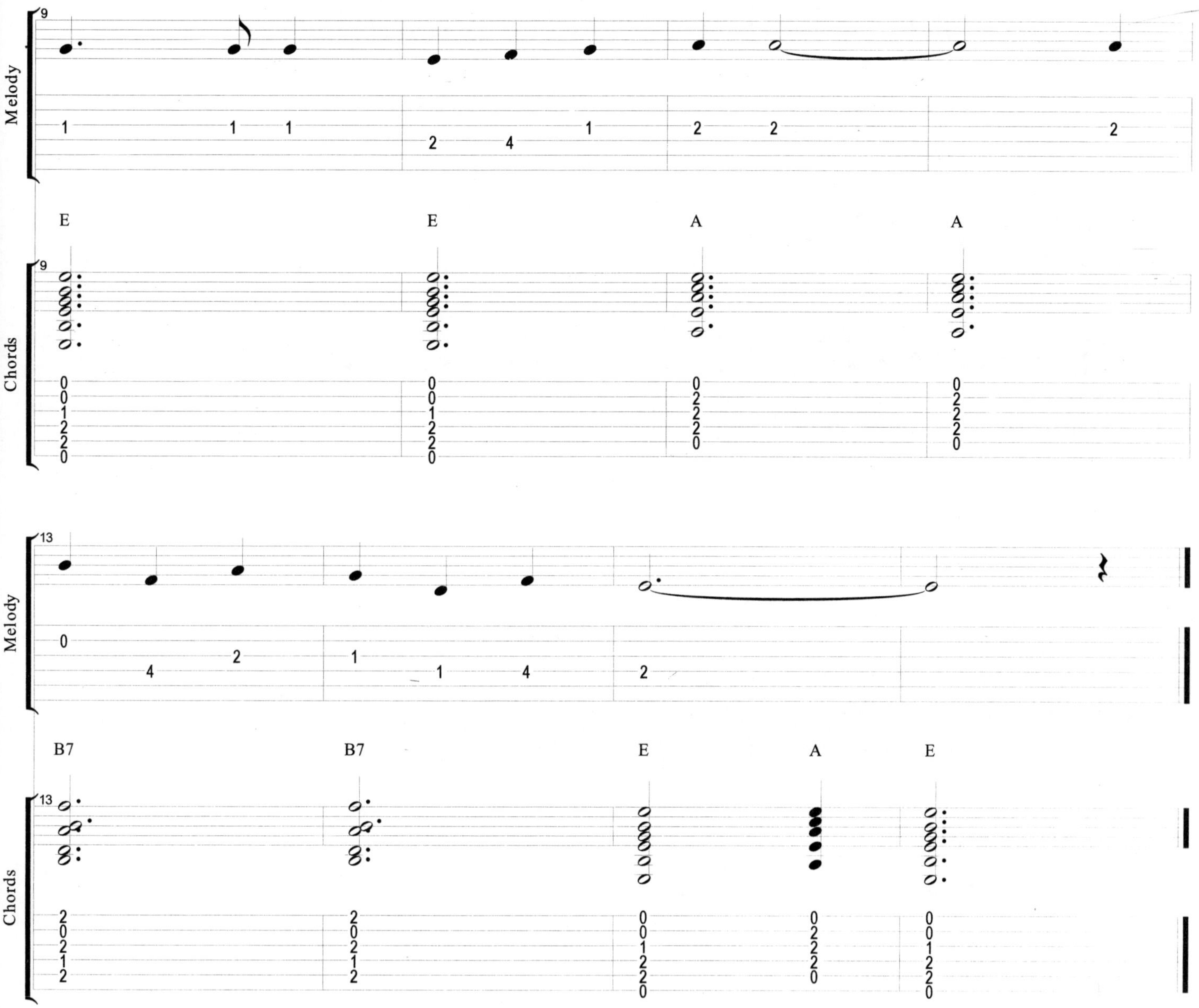
Melody
E
E
A
A
Chords
Melody
B7
B7
E
A
E
Chords

Go Tell It On The Mountain

Plectrum Guitar, Guitarmonk

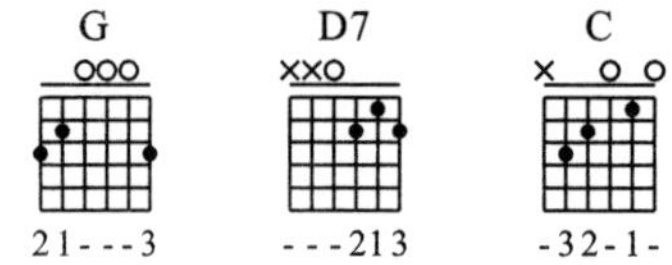

Moderate ♩ = 100

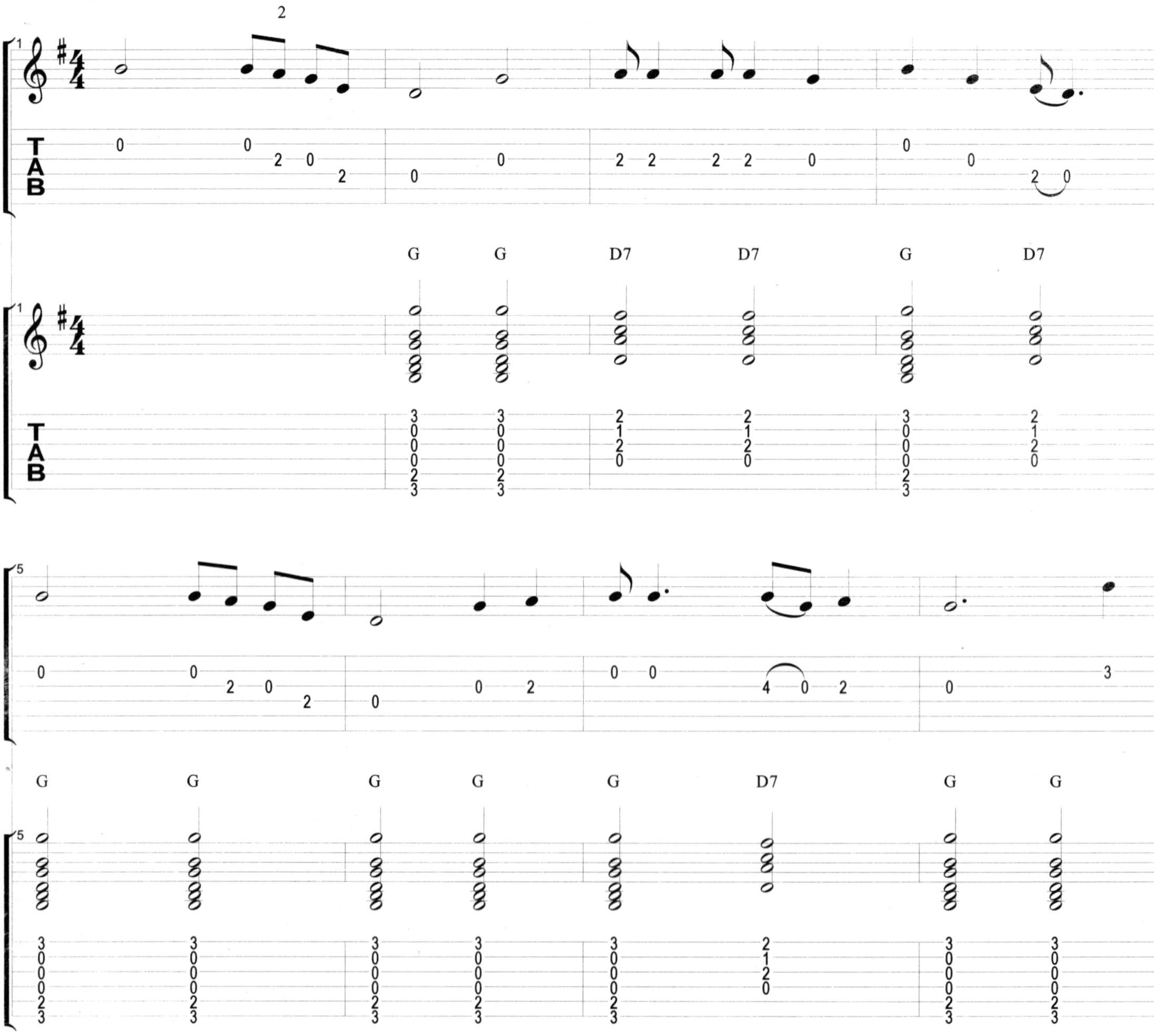

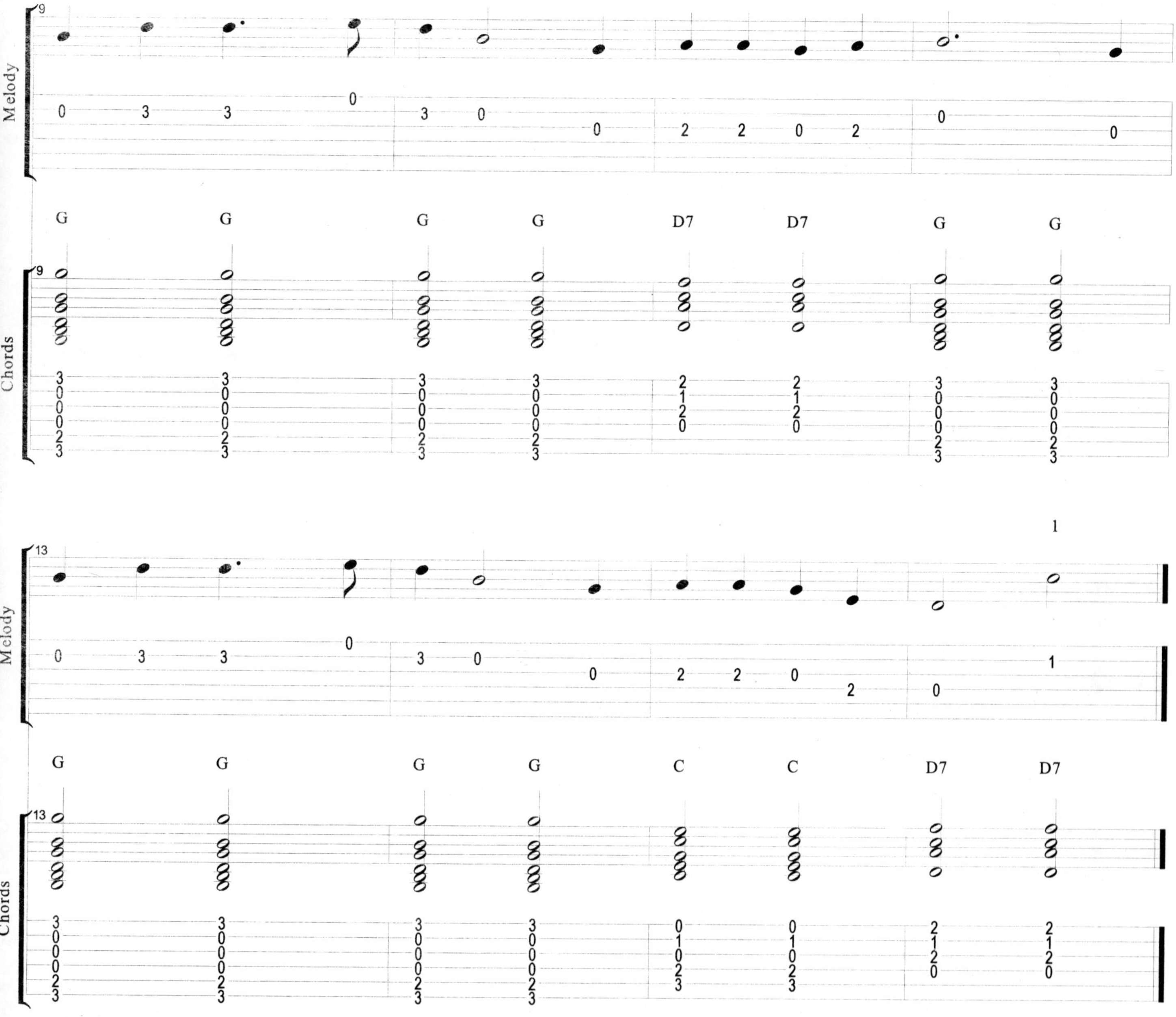
Melody
Chords
G G G G D7 D7 G G
Melody
Chords
G G G G C C D7 D7

Titan

Plectrum Guitar, Guitarmonk

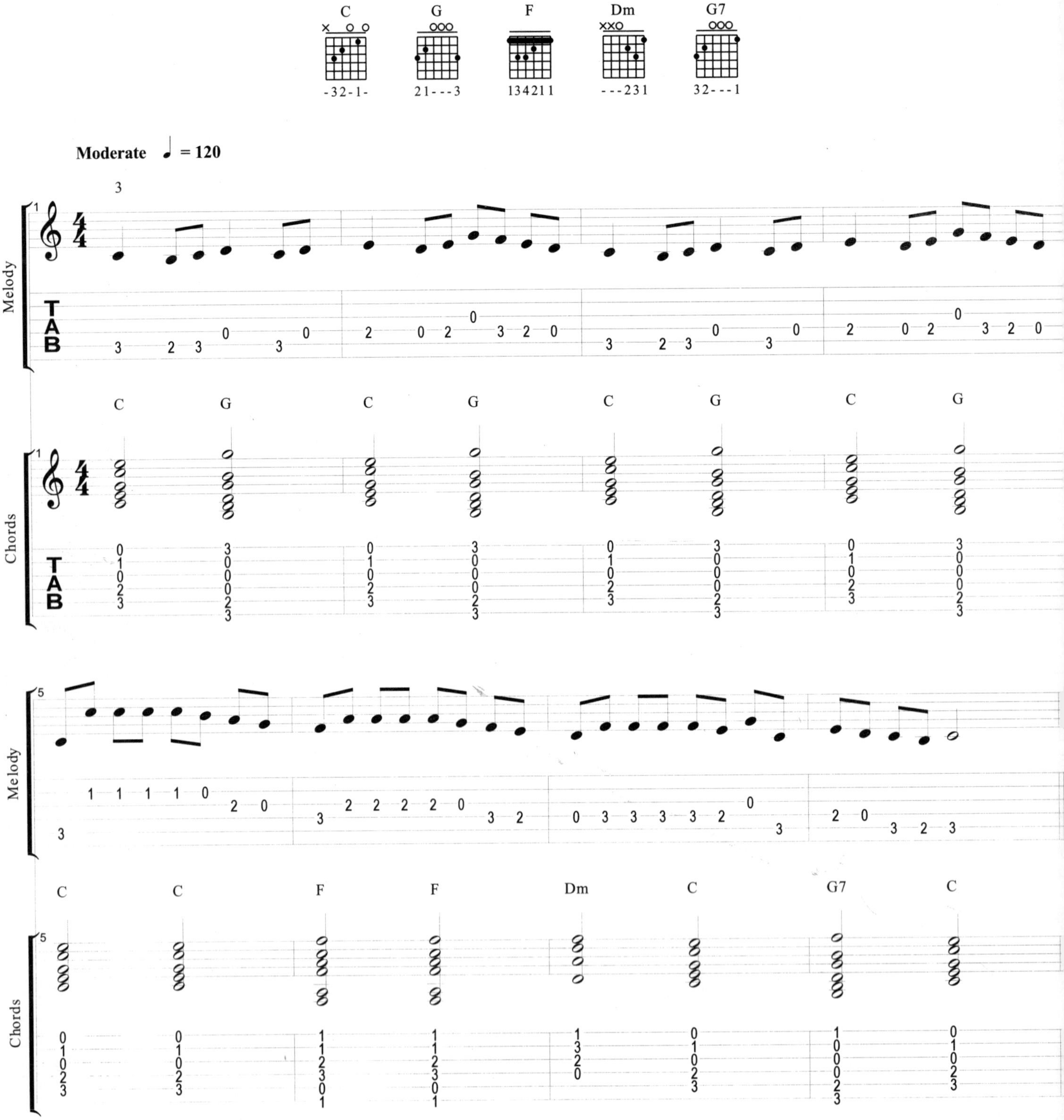

Long Long Ago

Plectrum Guitar, Guitarmonk

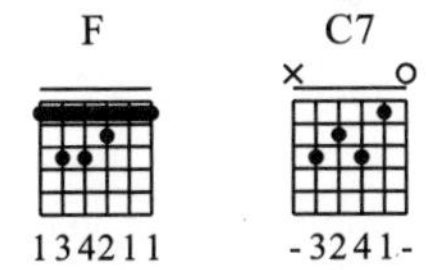

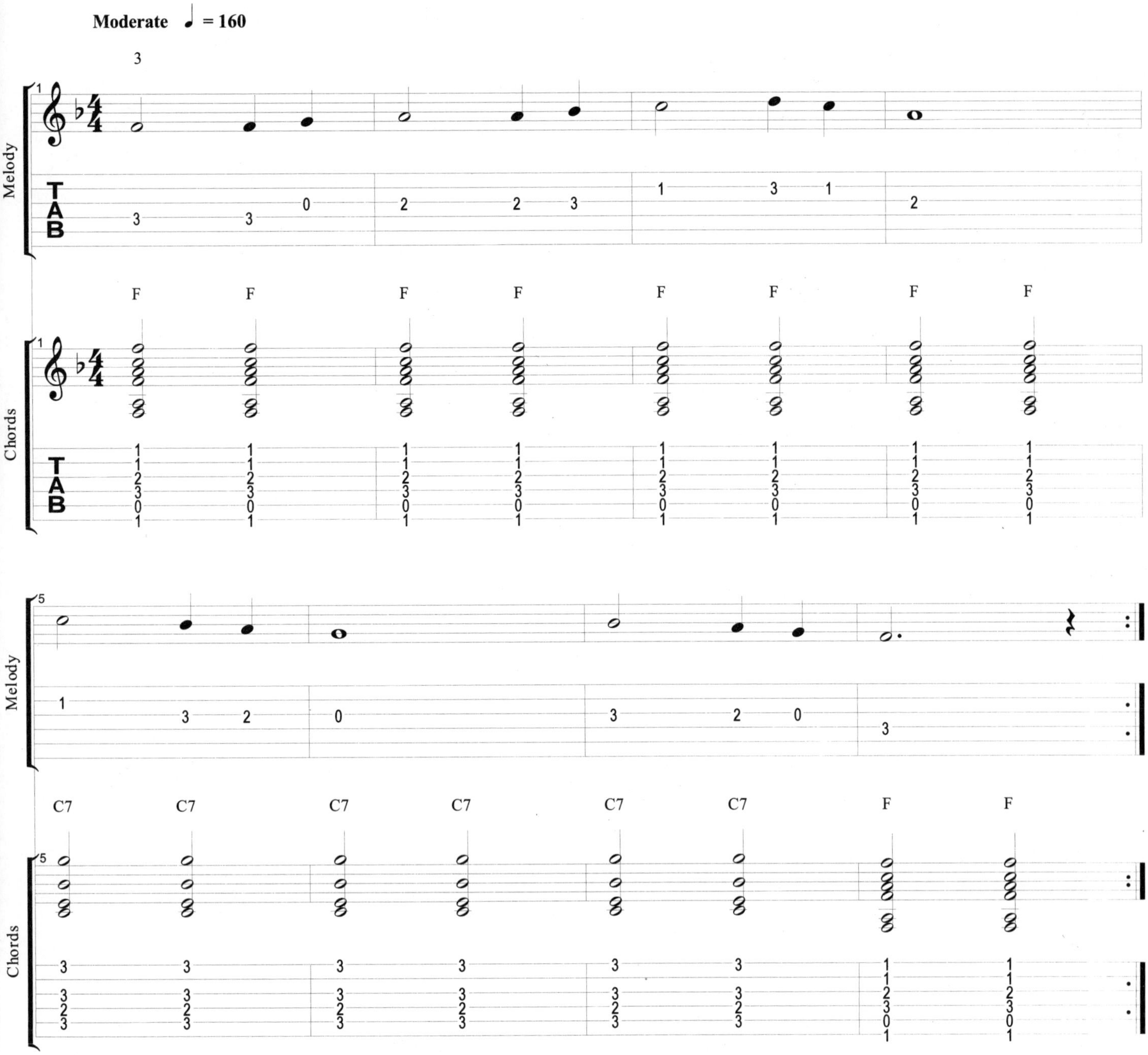

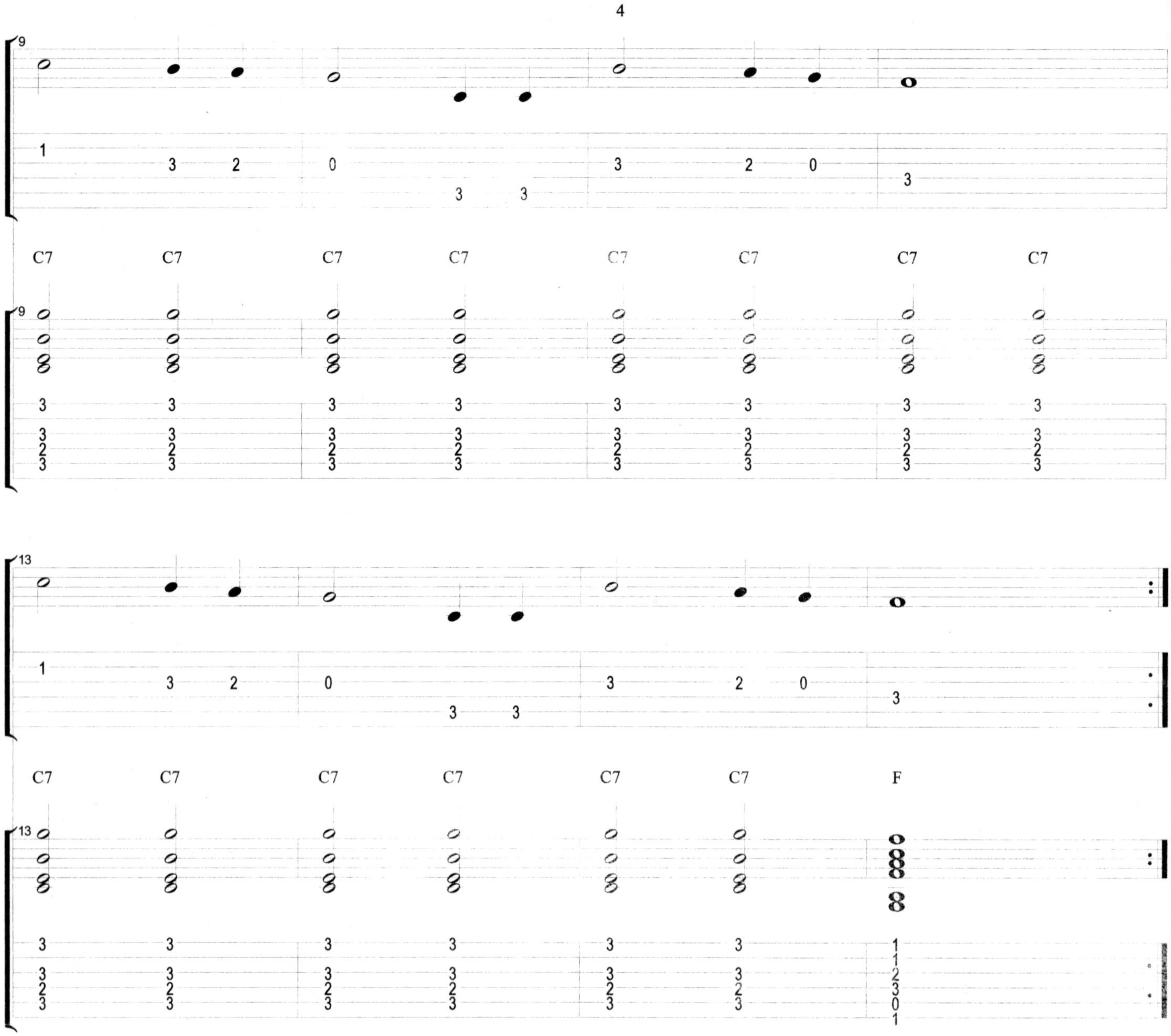
Melody
Chords
C7 C7 C7 C7 C7 C7 C7 C7
Melody
Chords
C7 C7 C7 C7 C7 C7 F

The Girl I Left Behind Me

Plectrum Guitar, Guitarmonk

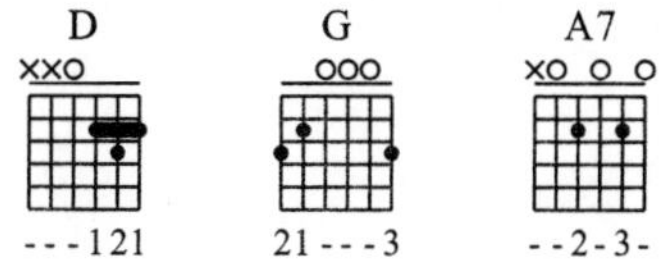

Moderate ♩ = 120

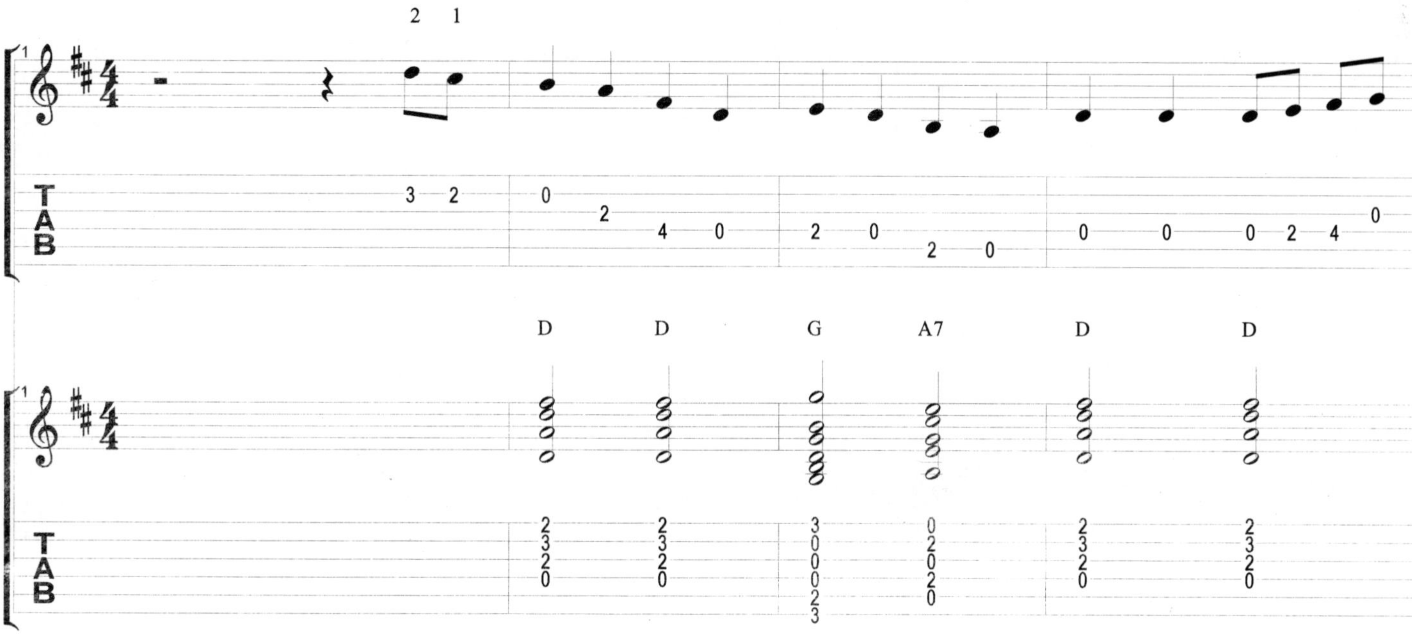

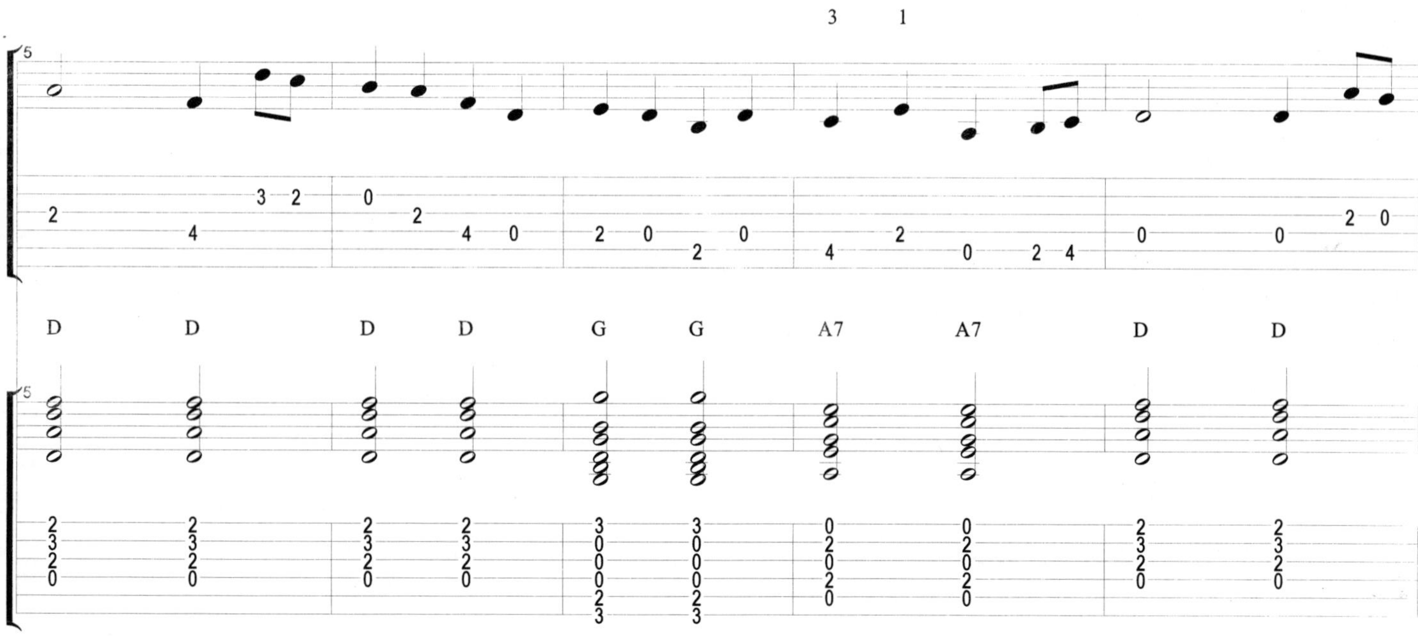

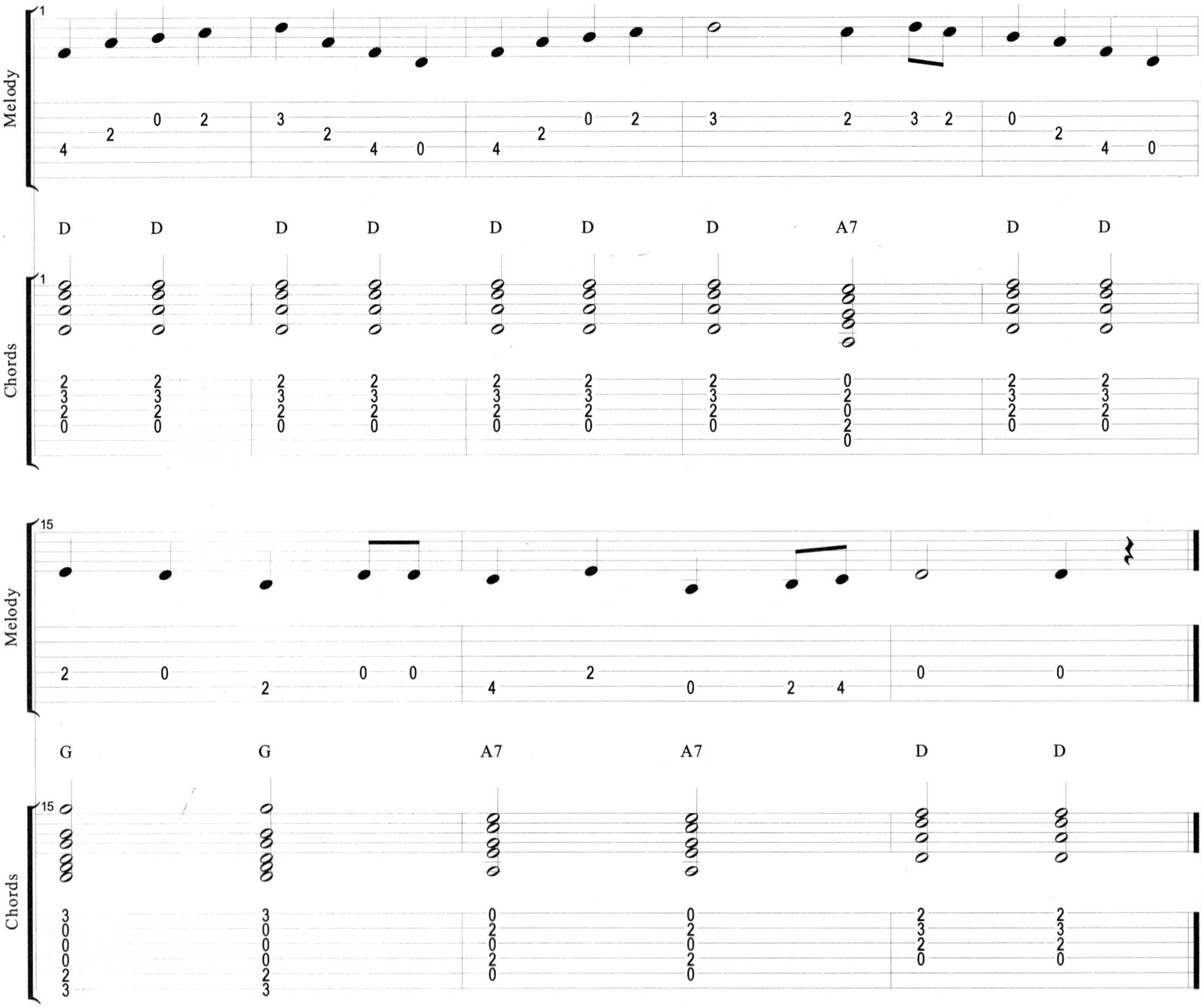
Melody
Chords
D D D D D D D A7 D D
Melody
Chords
G G A7 A7 D D

O Suzanna

Plectrum Guitar, Guitarmonk

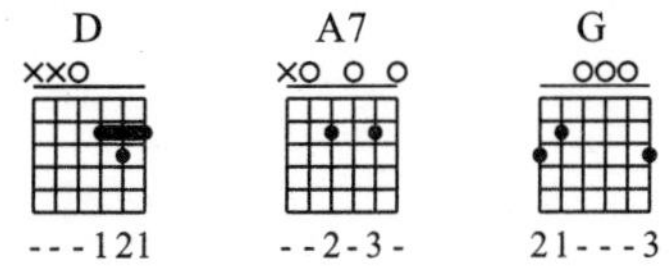

Moderate ♩ = 110

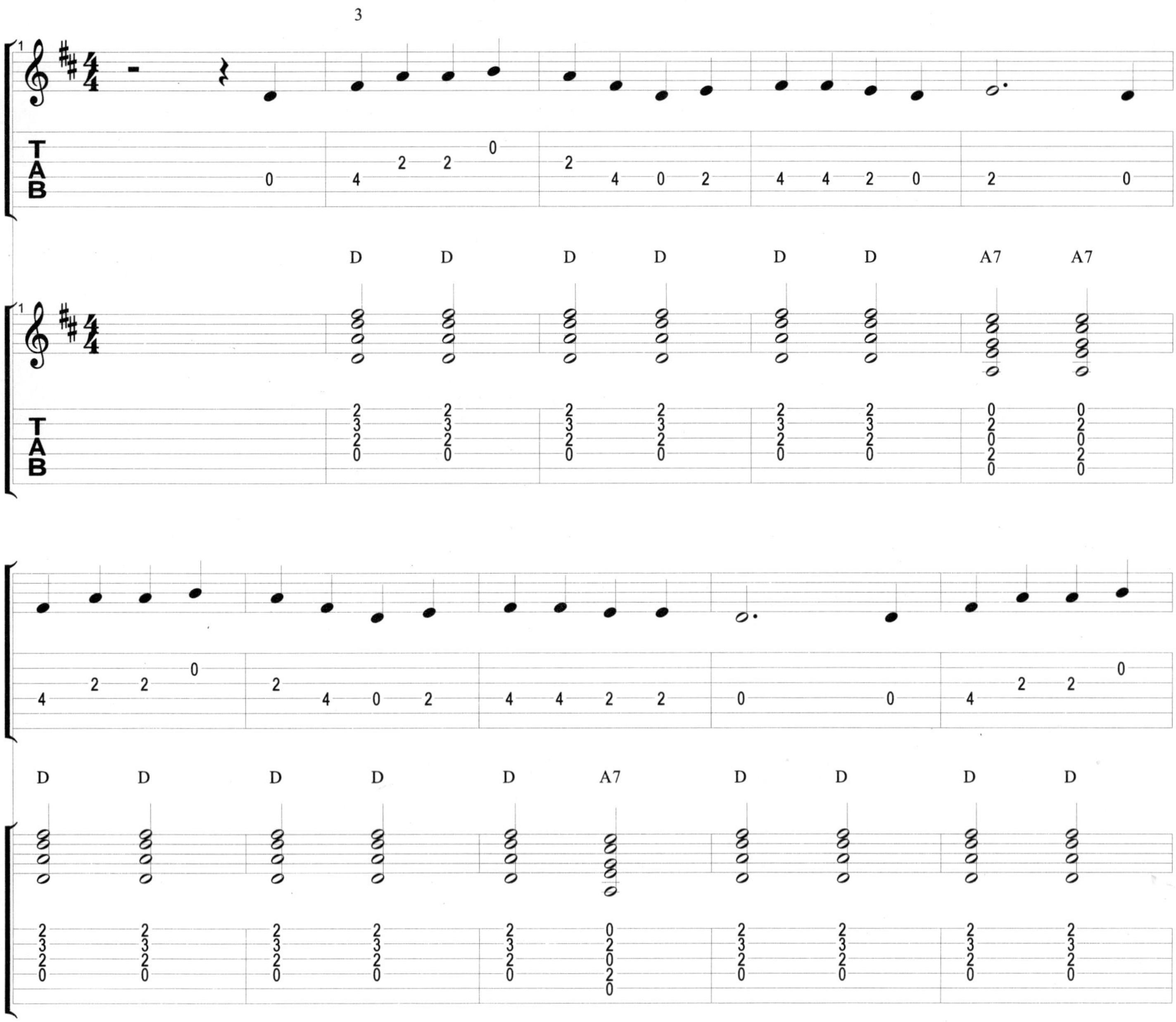

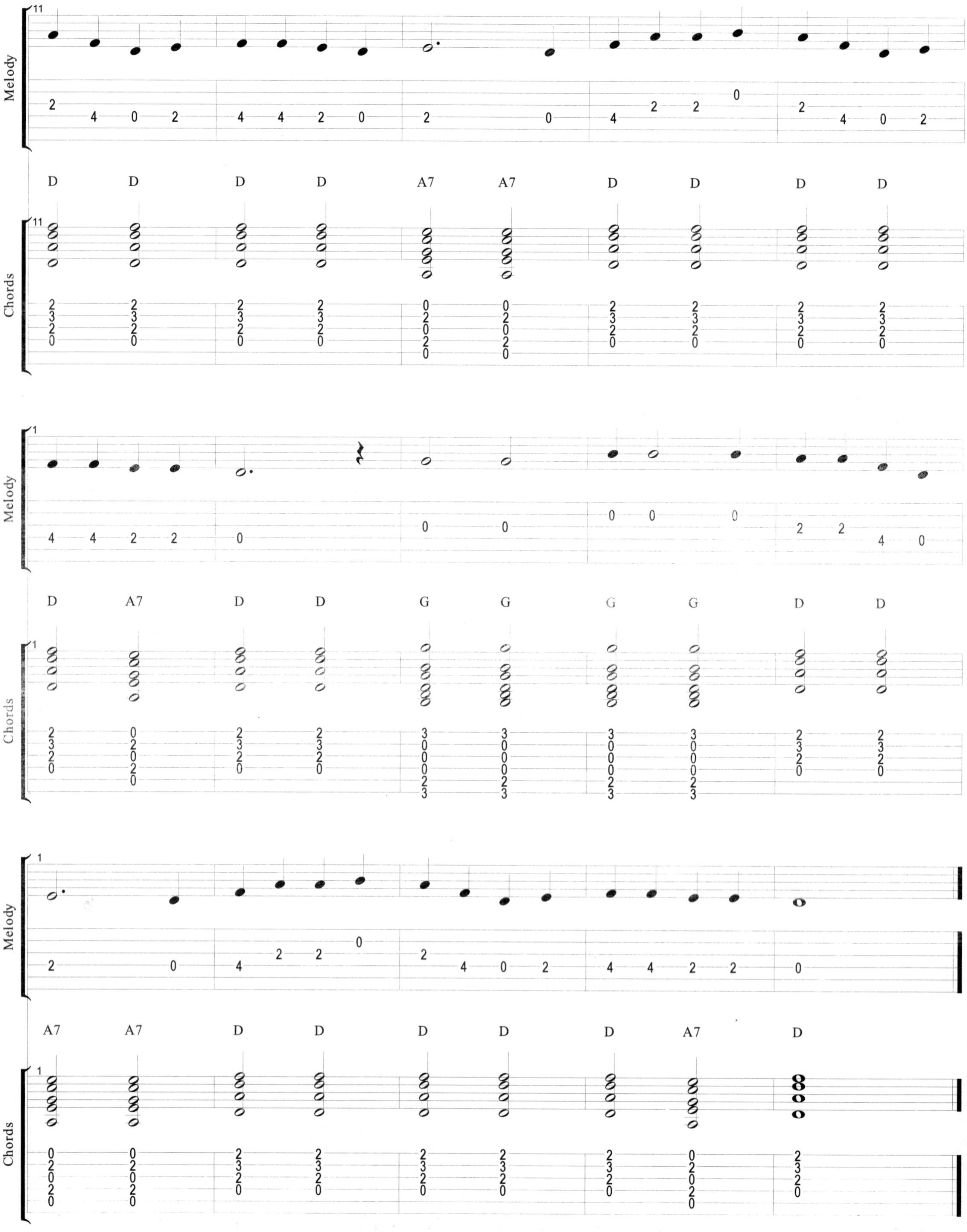
Melody
D D D D A7 A7 D D D D
Chords
Melody
D A7 D D G G G G D D
Chords
Melody
A7 A7 D D D D D A7 D
Chords

Amazing Grace

Plectrum Guitar, Guitarmonk

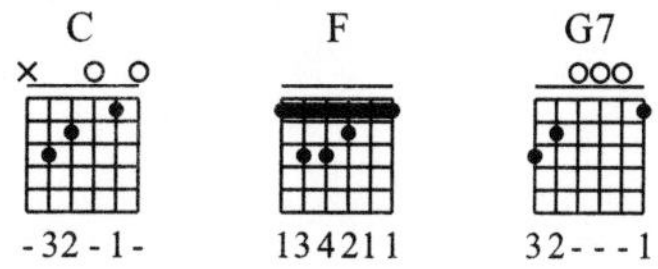

Moderate ♩ = 106

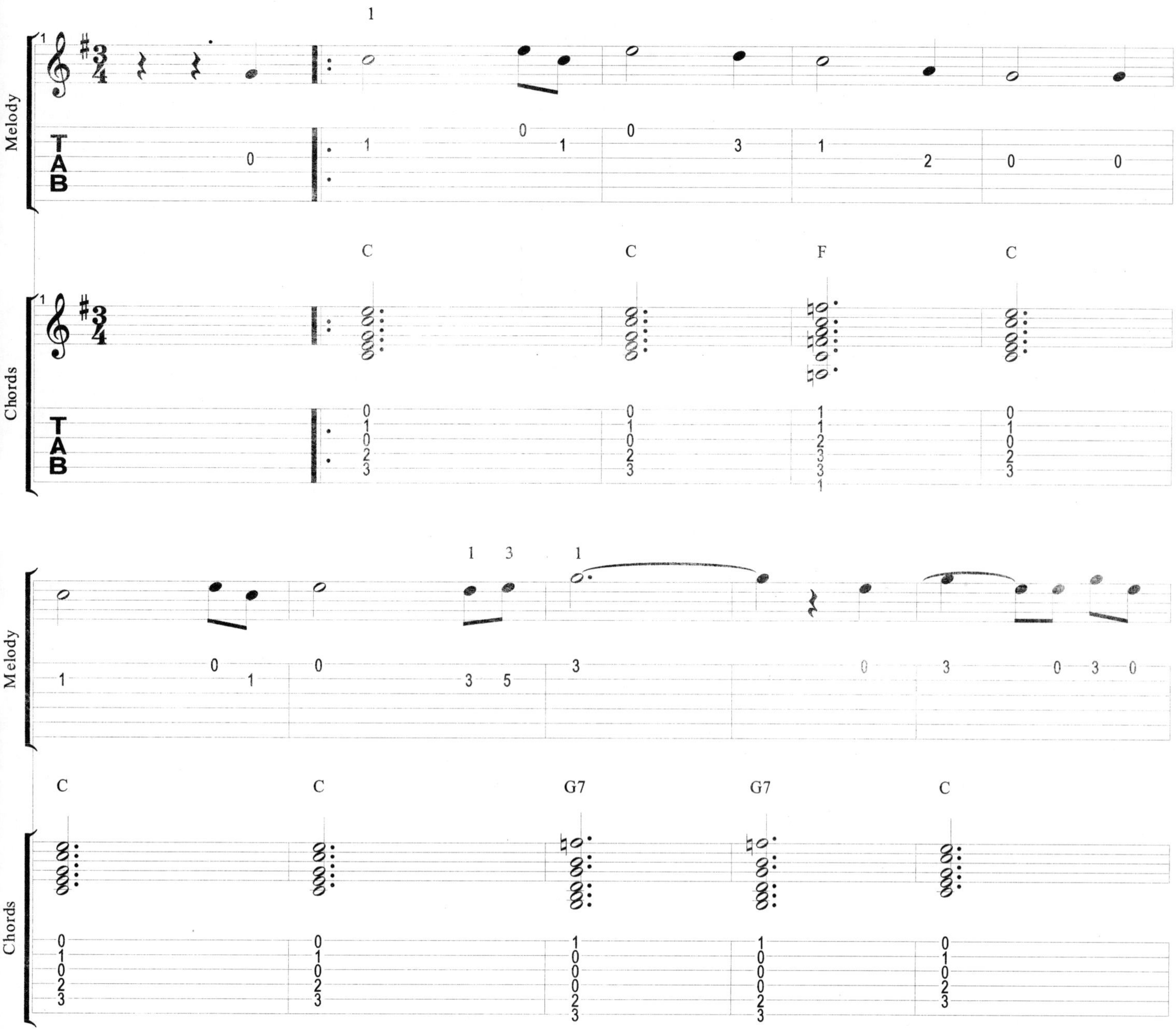

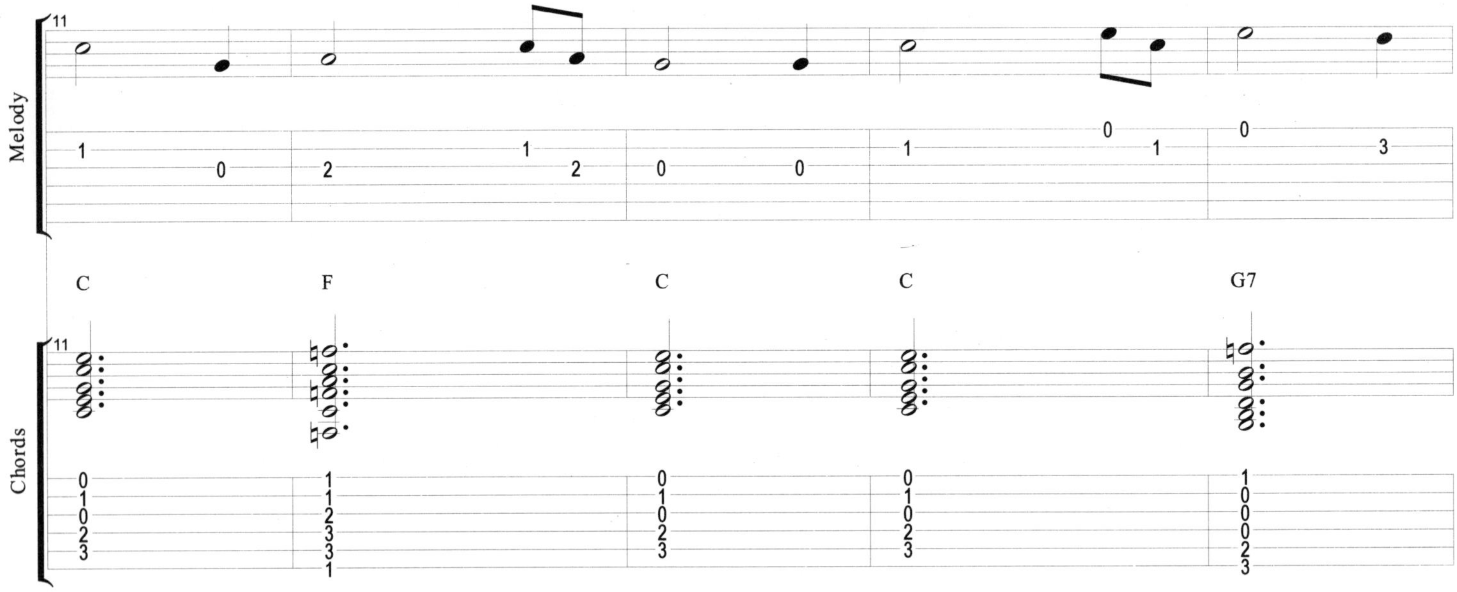
Melody
Chords
C
F
C
C
G7

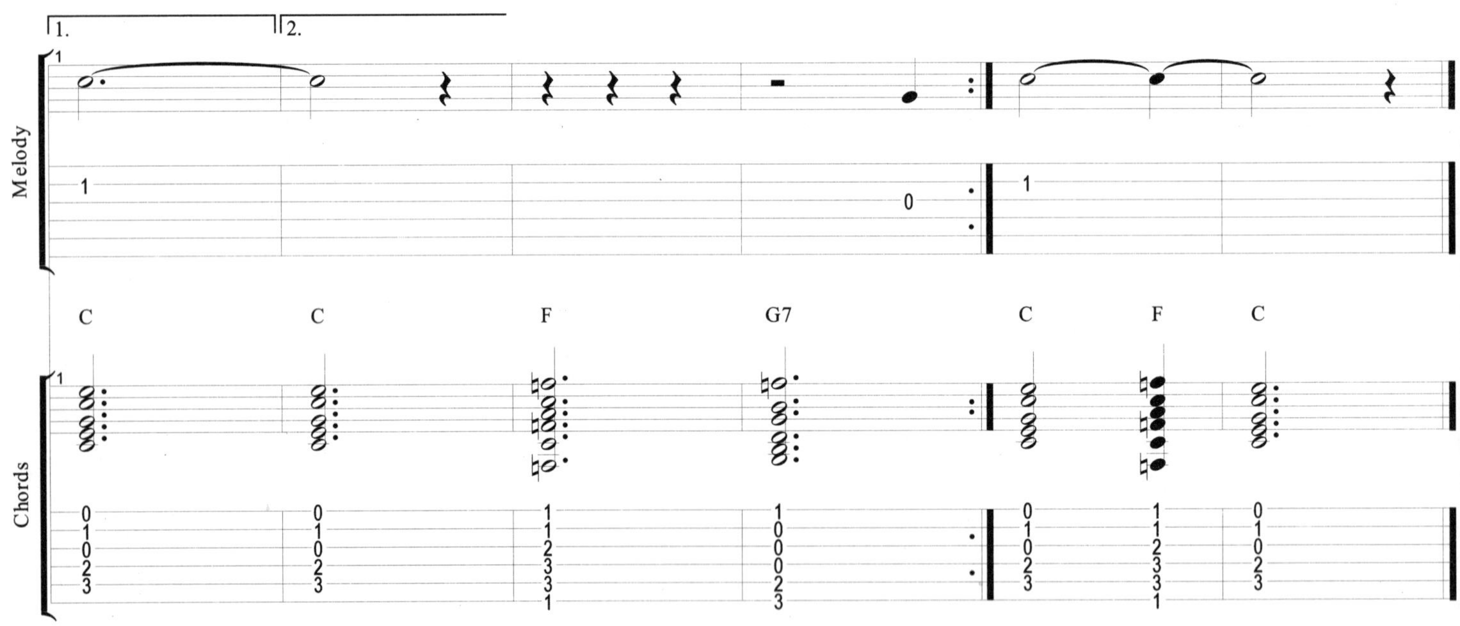
1.
2.
Melody
Chords
C
C
F
G7
C
F
C

500 Miles

Plectrum Guitar, Guitarmonk

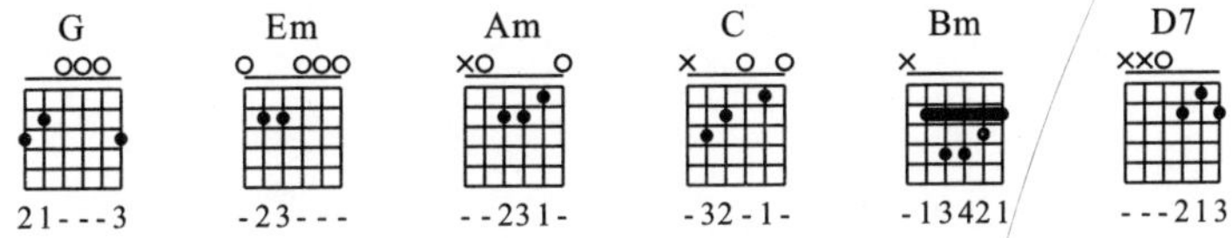

Moderate ♩ = 100

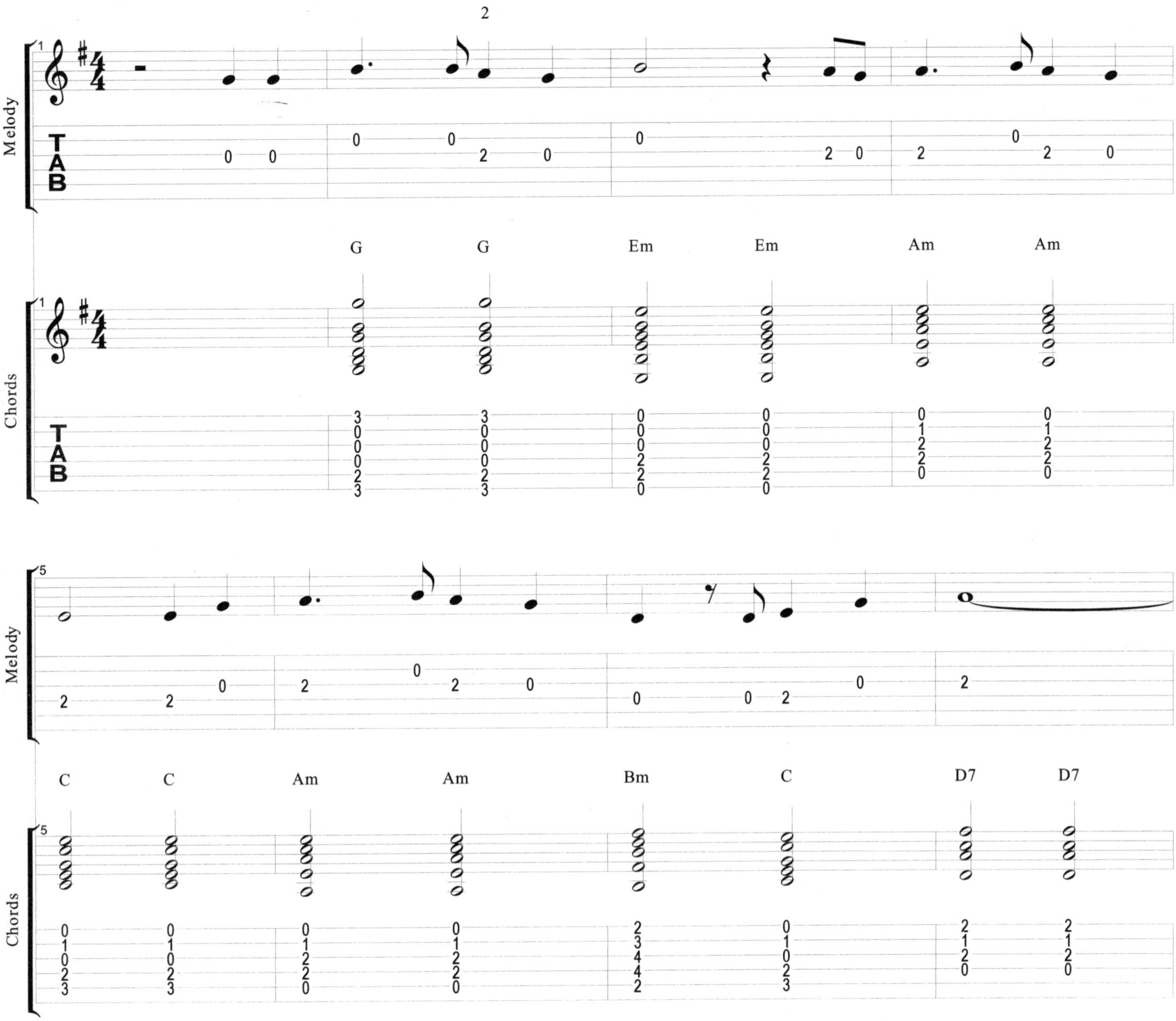

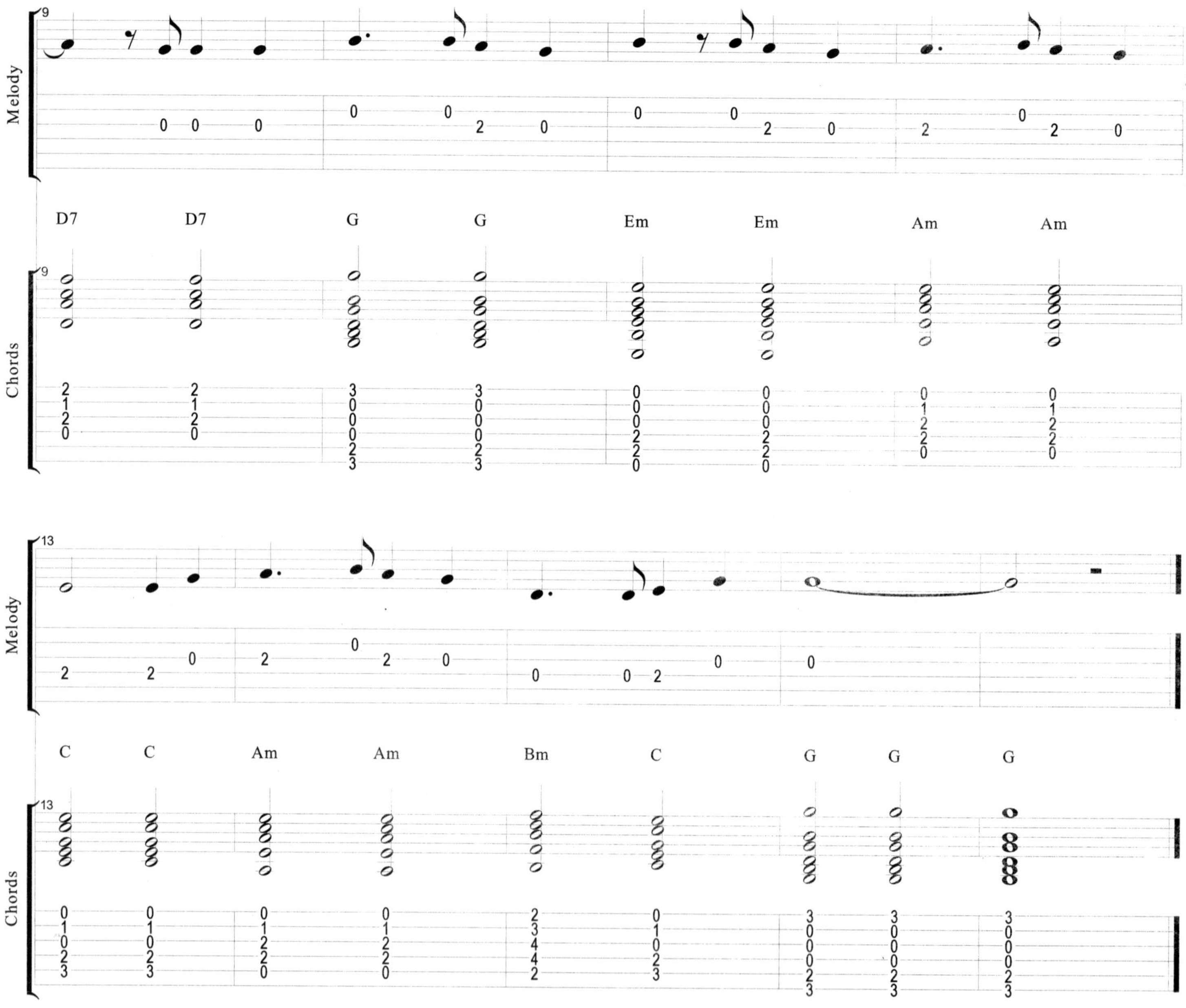
9
Melody
D7 D7 G G Em Em Am Am
Chords
13
Melody
C C Am Am Bm C G G G
Chords

Western Pop Songs

MUSIC CHORDS AND LYRICS

(A beautiful repertoire for all music lovers and students...)

WESTERN SONGS

1. Everything I do
2. Words
3. My heart will go on
4. Back to you
5. Right here waiting
6. Unbreakable
7. Truly Madly Deeply
8. I Need you

EVERYTHING I DO

1

Artist: Bryan Adams
Album: Waking up the Neighbour
Scale: Eb Major

```
Eb                          Bb
Look into my eyes, you will see,
Ab               Bb
What you mean to me,
             Eb                 Bb
Search your heart; search your soul,
             Ab                     Bb
And when you find me there you'll search no more..
      Fm                           Bb
Don't tell me it's not worth trying for,
         Ab                          Bb
You can't tell me; it's not worth dying for,
             Eb                Bb          Eb
You know it's true... Everything I do, I do it for you,

Eb                            Bb
Look into my heart, you will find,
Ab                      Bb
There's nothing there to hide
Eb                      Bb
Take me, as I am, take my life.
       Ab               Bb
I would give it, I would sacrifice,

Fm                                   Bb
Don't tell me it's not worth fighting for
      Ab                         Bb
I can't help it; it's nothing I want more.
           Eb                  Bb          Eb
You know it's true... Everything I do, I do it for you.

                      Fm                            Bb
Oh! Yeah! You can't tell me it's not worth trying for,
      Fm                           Bb
I can't help it; it's nothing I want more,
        Eb           Bb
Yeah! I'll fight for you, I die for you,
      Ab
Walk the wire for you
      Abm
Yeah! I die for you
           Eb                    Bb          Eb
You know it's true... Everything I do, I do it for you.
```

There's no love;
like your love,

And no other could,
give me more love,

There's no way,
unless you are there,

All the time,
all the way...

You know it's true,
Everything I Do...

WORDS

Artist: Boyzone
Album: A Different Beat
Scale: G Major

```
G
Smile an everlasting smile,
                              A
A smile can bring you near to me,
       D
Don't ever let me find you gone,
                              C       G
Cause that would bring a tear to me
```

```
    Bb
This world has lost its glory,
                                 F
Let's start a brand new story now, my love
    Bb
You think that I don't even mean,
                D
A single word I say,
       G                        D
It's only words and words are all I have,
                   G
To take your heart away,
```

```
G
Talk in everlasting words,
                    A
and dedicate them all to me
    D
and I will give you all my life
                        C     G
I'm there if you should call on me
```

Smile an everlasting Smile,

A smile can bring you,

Near to Me,

Don't ever let me find that

You are gone,

Cause that would bring a,

Tear to me...

MY HEART WILL GO ON

3

Artist: Celine Dion
Album: Titanic
Scale: E Major

```
E                  A              E          B
Every night in my dreams I see you I feel you,
E               A               B
That is how I know you go on.
E                  A              E          B
Far across the distance and spaces between us,
E                     A          B
You have come to show you go on.

E     B      A            B
Near far wherever you are,
   E               A            B
I believe that the heart does go on
 E    B         A        B
Once more you open the door,
            E                   B
And you're here in my heart,
       A            B       E
And my heart will go on and on

E                        A          E          B
Love can touch us one time and last for a life time
E               A               B
And never let go till we're gone
E                 A             E          B
Love was when I loved you, one true time I hold to,
E                A       B
In my life we'll always go on

Fm    Eb             Db       Eb
 Your here, there's nothing I fear
       Fm            Eb           Db Cm Bbm
 And I know that my heart will go on
Fm    Eb     Db       Eb
 We'll stay forever this way
         Fm       Eb
 You are safe in my heart
         Db            Eb       Fm Eb Db
 And my heart will go on and on
```

Every night in my dreams,

I see you, I feel you,

That I how I know you,

go on,

Far across the distance,

And spaces between us,

You have come to show,

you go on,

BACK TO YOU

Artist: Bryan Adams
Album: Unplugged
Scale: C Major

C   Am
I've been down, I've been beat,
F   Gsus4
I've been so tired that I couldn't speak,
C   Am
I've been so lost that I could not see,
F   Gsus4
I wanted things that were out of reach,
C   Am
Then I found you, and you helped me through,
F   Gsus4
And you showed me what to do,
F   E
That's why, I'm coming back to you,
Am   F   Gsus4   G
Like a star that guides a ship, across the ocean,
Am   F   Gsus4   G
That's how your love can take me home, back to you,
Em   Am   Em   Am
And if I wish upon that star, that someday I'll be where you are
F   Gsus4   G
I know that day is coming soon; yeah I'm coming back to you,

C   Am   F   Gsus4

Am   F   Gsus4   G

G   Am   F   Gsus4
I'm coming back to you
G   Am   F   Gsus4
I'm coming back to you
G   Am   F   Gsus4
I'm coming back to you
G   Am   F   Gsus4
I'm coming back to you
G   Am   F   Gsus4
That day is coming soon
G   Am   F   Gsus4
I'm coming back to you
G   Am   F   C/G

I've been down,

I've been beat,

I've been so tired that I

Couldn't see,

I wanted things that were,

Out of reach...,

RIGHT HERE WAITING

Artist: Richard Marx
Album: Repeat Offender
Scale: C Major

```
C         F                Dm
Oceans apart day after day
        G7           C
And I slowly go insane
C              F              Dm
I hear your voice on the line
      G/B                Am
But it doesn't stop the pain
               F
If I see you next to never
Am               Dm          G7
How can we say forever?

   C              F               Dm
I took for granted, all this times,
        G7                              C
That I thought would last somehow
C             F                         Dm
I hear the laughter, I taste the tears
      G/B                         Am
But I can't get you near you now
                    F
Oh, can't you see it baby
Am                      Dm          G7
   You've got me goin' crazy...

C                    G    E7           Am
Wherever you go, whatever you do,
                  F       G7              C
I will be right here waiting for you.
  C                   G                        E7     Am
Whatever it takes or how my heart breaks,
                  F             G7         Am
I will be right here waiting for you.
```

I wonder how we can survive this romance,

But in the end if I'm with you,

I will take the chance,

Wherever you go, whatever you do,

I will be right here waiting for you...,

UNBREAKABLE

6

Artist: Westlife
Album: Unbreakable
Scale: G Major

```
G                                  Em
Took my hand, touch my heart,
            C                 D
Held me close, you were always there,
          G              Em
By my side, night and day,
               C       D
Through it all, baby come what may,
         Em                          G
Swept away on a wave of emotion,
            C                                G
We were caught in the eyes of the storm,
         Em                               G                         Am
And whenever you smile I can hardly believe that you're mine
                         D
Believe that you're mine...
```

Share the Laughter, share the tears,
We both know, we will go on from here,
Cause together, we are strong,
In my arms that's where you belong,
I have been touched by the hands of an angel,
I have been blessed by the power of the love
And whenever you smile I can hardly believe that you're mine
Believe that you're mine...

This love is unbreakable,

It's unmistakable and each time I look in your eyes, I know why...,

This love is untouchable,

A feeling my heart just can't deny and each time I look in your eyes oh baby,

I know why...,

This love is Unbreakable...

```
                  G                      Em
This love is unbreakable, it's unmistakable
               C                              D
Each time I look in your eyes, I know why
                  G                            Em
This love is untouchable, a feeling my heart just can't deny
                  C                        G            D
Each time I look in your eyes, oh baby, I know why
                   Em
This love is unbreakable
```

TRULY MADLY DEEPLY

7

Artist: Darren Hayes
Album: Savage Garden
Scale: C Major

```
C                                       G
I'll be your dream, I'll be your wish I'll be your fantasy.
F                                   G
I'll be your hope; I'll be your love be everything that you need.
C                                   G
I love you more with every breath truly madly deeply do..
F                              G
I will be strong I will be faithful 'coz I'm counting on
C                    G
A new beginning, a reason for living
F                         G
A deeper meaning

C                                       G
And when the stars are shining brightly in the velvet sky,
F                                   G
I'll make a wish send it to heaven then make you want to cry,
C                                   G
The tears of joy for all the pleasure and the certainty,
F                              G
That we're surrounded by the comfort and protection of the
C                    G
Highest power, in lonely hours
F                         G
The tears devour you.

            C                            G
I want to stand with you on a mountain.
            F                         G
I want to bathe with you in the sea.
            C                  G
I want to lay like this forever.
            F                  G
Until the sky falls down on me
```

I'll be your dream,

I'll be your wish,

I'll be yourfantasy,

I'll be your hope,

I'll be your love,

Be everything that you need,

I NEED YOU

Artist: Mark Anthony
Album: Mended
Scale: C Major

```
C
From the day that I met you girl
                        G
I knew that your love would be
                F                         C
Everything that I ever wanted in my life
                                C
From the moment you spoke my name
                G
i knew everything had changed
                F                                  C
Because of you I felt my life would be complete
```

Nothing matters but you my love and

Only God above could be the one to know

Exactly how I feel

I could die in your arms right now,

Knowing that you somehow

Would take my soul and keep it deep inside your heart

Oh baby

```
F G   C
I need you
C
To make everything right girl
F G  C
I love you
C
And I'll never deny that
F G   C
I need you
```

Oh baby

I need you

For the rest of my girl

I need you

Say that you'll be my life,

I love you, wont you marry me, marry me.

I need you

I need you...